PROFESSOR JOHNSON UNHINGED:

Lectures on Teaching, Parenting and Student Violence

Bill Hoatson

by:
Bill Hoatson

Published by: SokheChapke Publishing, Inc.

This book is dedicated to anybody that has ever worked in a school system, from the administration all the way down to the teacher, and everybody in between.

Bill Hoatson

Professor Johnson Unhinged. Copyright © 2007 by Bill Hoatson. All Rights Reserved. Printed in the United States of America. No part of this book may be used or reproduced in any manner whatsoever without written permission except in the case of brief quotations embodied in critical reviews.

All characters and events depicted herein are purely fictional, any resemblance to persons living or dead, or actual events, is coincidental.

SokheChapke
"............not your mainstream publisher"
P.O. Box 21161
Tallahassee, FL 32316

CONTENTS

Introduction i
Book One
Addressing Teachers...1
So, You Want To Be A Teacher? 5
So, You Still Want To Be A Teacher? 37

Book Two
Addressing Students..65
Professor Johnson's Screed Against Violence 67
Forward: Parenting Lecture...103
Professor Johnson's Infamous Lecture on Parenting 107

INTRODUCTION

This is an unexpected introduction. I am writing it in the hopes that my publisher will stop disfiguring herself. She is a beautiful African American woman who is a genius. She is also, as I write, yanking hands full of hair out of her head and has probably chewed her fingernails down to the second knuckle by now. Not liking her new look, her equally brilliant and understanding husband is probably on the way over to beat me up, so I am writing quickly.

She loves what I do, but the fear is always there that I am going to be too "edgy", which is her favorite adjective. Instead of treading softly, as she is urging me to do, she often looks over and sees me doing the Highland Fling in places of the American experience where I am not really even supposed to be.

I am a white guy of Scottish descent, from an upper middle class background. I am a firm believer that God puts you where he wants you. God put me in the most beautiful rural county in Florida. It is a mosaic populated by great people: 57% are black, 36% are white, and 7% are Hispanic.

God also gives you something to do. You can call it destiny. The Hindu's call it Dharma. I am a teacher. Always have been, always will be.

Many of the wonderful people in this county are mired in the quicksand of grinding poverty with all of it's brutal ramifications, including dysfunctional family units feeding into a sometimes dysfunctional school system. My job is to save and empower as many of my children and my families as I can. I believe that a good education is the way out of the bog. I have spent thirty years fighting for MY children. If you don't believe that the children you receive in your classroom every day are a personal gift from God, no matter the color of their faces, the language they speak, their gender, or their behavior, then burn your teacher's certificate and do something worthwhile, like amassing mountains of money.

I live at an intersection in the switching yard of race, religion, poverty, wealth, politics, power, and culture. What a glorious train wreck it is, what we call the American public school system, and it has made my life rich.

Besides, dysfunction is a gold mine for humor. I know that God has a sense of humor. If you are a school teacher you better have one, too. It is more important than chalk.

So, I don't think I'm going to change a word of what I wrote. These are the stories of my children and my families. These are my stories. My publisher will understand. Like I said, she is a genius. To put her at ease, think about buying my other book, a play called "Mr. Harrison's Classroom: A Documentary". Maybe she will call her husband back before he gets here.

Bill Hoatson

BOOK ONE
ADDRESSING TEACHERS

Professor Johnson taught in public schools for decades before he went to the college level, as well as having a career as a consultant, speaker, and writer. In his later years he loved to go back and speak to teachers. He got a genuine kick out of it, likening his tours to that of Bob Hope entertaining the troops. The comparison is not that far fetched. In the Professor's eyes many teachers, like their soldier counterparts, find themselves on the front line, underfunded, meshed in bloated bureacracies, powerless to make policy, all the while getting hammered from a dozen different directions. They also, like their soldier counterparts, are worth their weight in gold and deserve better.

If any profession needs entertainment to relieve stress, it is teaching. Professor Johnson called it **VENTERTAINMENT** and appeared to enjoy every second of it. He figured that, if nothing else, it was cheaper than therapy.

Preface

"So, You Want To Be A Teacher?" is a lecture that Professor Johnson gave to the 2003 graduating class at Wolverton's Teachers College.

SO, YOU WANT TO BE A TEACHER?

Well, it's wonderful to see everybody tonight. Those people in the back are my veteran teachers. Experience has taught them to sit as close to the exit as possible. There's no telling how boring a faculty meeting may be, so they're going to hug the escape hatch real tight. But to the eager new ones down in front, I want to welcome you to a noble profession. So, you want to be a teacher? Good for you. I know of no higher calling, which leaves me a little puzzled. I read some scary statistics the other day. The average regular- ed teacher lasts only three and one half years. Think about that. Three and a half years!

I studied that statistic for awhile. I think that the fraction one-half is the key to understanding here. The first year is spent in full-tilt survival mode. The second year goes a little better, so you think that you are starting to get a handle on it. By the end of the third year you are doing well enough to start to concentrate on other things, like the fact that you can't pay your bills and they have repossessed your car while your back was turned because you were on the phone with an angry parent. So, evidently, it dawns on the teacher sometime during their Christmas break of the following year that, "HEY, I'M OUT OF HERE." That's the reason why other jobs don't give those long holidays. Way too much time for introspection.

The attrition rate leads me to think that there might be just a little disconnect between the realities of teaching and the college prep courses offered at universities. What kind of courses do you sign up for, exactly, to prepare you for all this?

I once signed up for a course called, "How to Write a Lesson Plan". I figured it's important and how hard could this be, anyway? The syllabus was four inches thick. I thought that maybe this was some cruel joke being played on us by the university. And I was right. Not only was it four inches thick, but it was so mind-numbingly boring that there is not enough coffee or amphetamines on this planet that could get you through even one page of it. Since college students are so eager and intense, I suppose they need something like this to bridle them back a bit, otherwise they'd never survive the faculty meetings, or those wonderful day-long workshops.

Sometimes college students are a little too intense for their own good. Ever see one during a lecture? They don't pay a lick of attention to it. They are too busy writing. They don't just take notes, they write down every single word. Why waste time filtering out the important stuff? I have seen gerbils less busy. After teaching for a couple of decades I was taking a course to keep my teacher's certificate current and found myself sitting in an auditorium with three hundred college students listening to a lecture on how to detect child abuse. They were all hunched over. You couldn't see their faces, just a sea of humped up backs. It was sort of like waiting to get a glimpse of a porpoise when it comes up for air, except in this case, they never do. I did see a hand come up once though. It came up to change the tape on this girl's machine. She was writing and recording at the same time. I'm thinking, "Oh, no, she's not." Then I thought, "Of course she is." She has to, because she didn't listen to one word of what the man was saying. I just hoped that she wasn't going to take notes at the house, too. For forty-five minutes every kid around me had been bent over, writing furiously. I hadn't moved my pen once. The professor was droning on, "If you happen to see burn marks on their arms or large bruises on their backs or chest, you need to report these......" Everybody was steadily writing. Finally, I couldn't take it anymore. I said to the girl sitting next to me, "Young lady, what are you doing?" "I'm taking notes." "Let me ask you this. If you had a child in your class who had cigarette burns and welts all over his body, what would you think?" "I'd think it was child abuse." "So, why are you writing it down?" A light went on in her head. You could see it shine through her eyes. "Well, I don't know." She put her pen down, sat back, and listened to the rest of the lecture, watching her hunched over classmates in amazement.

The next statistic I read was for special-ed teachers. They last, on average, three and a half days. What is up with that? Except you don't say special-ed, anymore. This labeling thing is tricky business and further proof, as if any is needed, that the powers that be often don't have a clear grasp of what they are doing. You'll learn a lot about the powers-that-be in this profession. Who are they? It's not YOU. That becomes immediately clear. You will never hear the word power and teacher in the same sentence. At least you won't have to worry yourself over decision making. Anyway, those in charge are not always, how shall we say, up to task.

Labeling. In order to get funding for a child with learning disabilities, you have to give them a label, which usually means scarring them for life. If you see a forty year old man ducking and hiding from other grown men in the soup isle of the grocery store, I'll bet you fifty dollars that he had been given some crazy label in school. Old habits are hard to break. Labeling seems a little too much like the rationale used in Vietnam. "Yes, colonel, if you give me enough napalm I can save the ENTIRE village." Destroy the child to save the child - I'm having a little trouble with that one. And you can tell that bureaucrats are uncomfortable with this labeling thing, because the labels keep changing. They started with "mentally retarded." Whew, that's a little harsh, don't you think? I don't know WHAT they were thinking about on that one. I mean, we're talking about a child here. Why don't we cut little Suzie a little slack? Then it was "mentally handicapped." I can see it right now. Right in the middle of the lecture on how every child has a bright future and can be anything they want to be when they grow up, a student stands up, goes to the dictionary and slowly thumbs through it. He's thinking, "Well, maybe handicapped doesn't mean what I thought it meant. Maybe it's something good." Slowly his finger goes down the page, then stops. "Uh-huh. Just what I thought," and slams the book shut. Actually, this handicapped label isn't necessarily all bad for him. Now he doesn't have to do any work. Chemistry? "No, I can't do that." Algebra? "No, I can't do that either. And I've got the papers to prove it!" So they had to pier six that one and came up with SPECIAL education instead. I don't know about you, but I know of very few teenagers who think being called special is a good thing. For one, it makes it almost impossible to get a date. For another, we're talking about a group of people who are so terrified of being different that they will pierce every possible body part with pieces of metal just to keep up with the Joneses. So now, instead of SPECIAL it's EXCEPTIONAL education. I would highly recommend that caffeine be outlawed at the Department of Education. It hops them up and makes them way too busy. Instead of resting on their laurels with the word "Exceptional", they're on a roll now, so they come up with "Gifted". Yes sir, Jimmy's very bright. Just put him in there with the other special, I mean exceptional, kids. Whatever. Just put them all in that empty room. We'll sort them out later.

The people that are yelling "teacher shortage, teacher shortage!" are like General Burnsides during the Battle of Fredericksburg. He sent wave after wave of young boys against an impregnable rebel wall to be slaughtered. At the end of the day his solution was to yell "soldier shortage!", without once asking, "what is happening to the soldiers that I've already got?" Three and a half years. What is happening to all those young, energetic teachers that WE'VE got? We need some practical stuff in some of those prep classes, like what to say when a student interrupts your class with

"BORING."

A lot of kids are bored these days. Ever notice that? "BORING." They'll say it right in the middle of "Saving Private Ryan." No understanding or respect for anything. No interest in learning anything. They're not bad kids. They're just too comfortable, that's all. And have very few life experiences. And even fewer goals. When I ask a student what they want to do for a living and they respond with, "stay in the bed", they are shocked to learn that this is not an occupation, much less a lucrative one. They don't understand that there is an alternative to living a life of comfort and ease. That there is an alternative to surviving. That, unless you have some real skills, poverty is not just an abstract concept. Even many of the kids living in poverty are shielded from the reality. Now, mom knows the reality of poverty. She works two full time jobs just to be able to afford the expensive brand of tuna. She just doesn't want Johnny to know. Now, some moms need to rethink the game plan. They come home and Johnny is laying on the couch with a new Gameboy, wearing shoes that cost more than a brand new set of snow tires, yelling "Where's the food?" I don't know about anybody else, but I would not treat my son like a prince, unless, in fact, he was one. Even then, I would demand to see a royal seal on a letter of proof.

Children are bored because they have no sense of history. They think that pushing a pencil across a piece of paper in an air conditioned room is work. They don't know that children were used in the mines because they had small fingers, which they would often lose, or that girls were chained to sewing machines twelve hours a day, or that many kids worked in the fields from sunup to sundown. They don't know that compulsory school laws were passed to prevent child abuse. So I use a little history to unbore them and when I see their hair standing on end I know that they are ready to do something productive without whining that their head hurts or the universal "I'm tired." Oh, are you now? From what, I often wonder? I guess that staying up all night on the internet lying to someone while they are lying to you is wearing on one. If a child threatens to drop out of school because it is too much boring work, let them. It will be a character building experience. Work construction in one hundred degree heat for a tobacco spitting guy with a buzz cut who calls you everything but your real name all day long. See if it doesn't get your mind right. It worked for me. After a year of that I discovered that I had the ability to be a straight A student. I would kiss the desk, then the floor, then the professor's feet, in that order, every time I entered the classroom. Real life is an attention getter.

Now, sometimes, I admit, it's not just the student's perception that is off. Some of it IS boring. Remember when you were bored in school? Don't do that to your students. The first thing you learn in med school is "Do no harm." Well, it's a great idea for teachers, too. I took this class once at a Junior College. I was going to be an inhalation therapist. The instructor was a retired nurse about two hundred years old. She taught by filmstrip. The first one she showed was thirty minutes long, an award winner called,

"How to Wash Your Hands." To make it even better, the picture and the record didn't match. For a half an hour we were treated to a poorly written comedy routine. In the next class it was "How to Read a Thermometer", which was even funnier when the pictures didn't match the sound. Better yet, I turned around to look at the teacher, expecting to see her napping, having been retired for eighty years and all, but she was wide awake, staring intently at the screen. I was stunned. This went on every class. It was so unbelievable that nobody wanted to spoil what was shaping up to be the most ridiculous class of all time. It would have been even funnier, except that it dawned on the kids whose parents weren't footing the bill that they themselves were actually paying hundreds of dollars for this. Talk about a bunch of wet blankets. It did teach me something, however. I knew that the medical profession was not for me. Not after seeing what it had done for this lady.

    Another time I took a class on reading disabilities. Although universities are a place of higher learning, I learned not to get too excited about a class just because it has a cool title. I found myself sitting with about thirty other professionals, all there to keep their various certificates up to date. Over a period of days and countless hours of prattling about everything under the sun BUT reading disabilities I realized I had boarded the HMS Bounty and it was going to be a very long voyage. My ears perked up once when he did mention the word reading, but it was only in the context of reading his watch in the dark that he had bought when he visited China. Tenure is not always a good thing. To make matters worse, the elderly ladies around me were trying desperately to make sense out of the class. Whenever one of them got up the courage to ask a question he would belittle them. This was not funny entertainment like the filmstrip class. More like watching Halloween IV: bad and gruesome. A pall of gloom hung over the room. Some of the ladies were worried that they weren't even going to get credit for their time in the torture chamber. I finally had enough. The next day, when I was getting ready to enter the class, I noticed four of the women standing outside the front door. One of them was crying. If this ever happens in your class it is probably a pretty good clue that you are not going to win teacher of the year. I decided it was time to give them what I regarded as sage advice. "Ladies, you need to do what I do. Drink a beer before class. Or two. This guy here seems like a six pack problem to me, but I don't want to see anybody falling out of their seat." At first they stared at me in disbelief. At least the woman wasn't crying anymore. Whoever said that laughter is the best medicine was Doctor Right On Target. Beer wasn't exactly to their taste but it didn't seem like they had any problem with wine, which is classier and healthier, anyway. Now, the lesson to all this is, if people have to resort to alcohol to combat boredom, that is definitely not a good sign. I am a firm believer that nothing happens to you without a reason, so actively try to remember your terrible classroom experiences. They were given to you for a reason. They are signposts of what *not* to do.

To combat boredom in the classroom, I

developed my "jaw dropper" theory of education, which came about, as do most flashes of brilliance, quite by accident. One day, many years into my teaching career, I was told that I had to teach science. I was an exceptional education teacher, which means that eventually you will have to teach any subject imaginable. Why? Because it's on your students' schedule, that's why. If it says Biosphere Design and Planning, then that's what you do. Just stick the kid next to the one who's taking remedial ceramics. I'm sure there's a common thread there somewhere. Every child has their own individualized education plan and you learn as a teacher to do what you are told, or you'll find yourself searching for employment at the local Waffle House. So I was told to teach science, which wouldn't have been too bad, except that I HATED science. If we step back for a second we might ponder how that is even humanly possible. How can somebody hate what is basically the study of every fascinating thing in the universe, including the study of life itself? The answer is obvious. You can't. You CAN develop a deep and abiding hatred for the idiot of a science TEACHER who turned you off to learning about your world in the first place, however. That is a much healthier attitude.

So, now I was stuck with teaching three times a day something for which I had absolutely no enthusiasm. I didn't even know where to begin. So I did what every teacher does in my situation. I referred to the textbook. That was a mistake. They were the "exceptional" version of science textbooks. They were even duller than the lesson plan syllabus from college, which I did not think was possible. After two days of using them I realized that I couldn't do this to these students for an entire year. The last forty-eight hours had already seemed like a year. I began to wrack my brain. The heck with the students now, I had to find something that interested ME. I have since gotten into all this new age physics, quantum physics, and string theory. If you can't find something in there that you find interesting, you are probably dead and don't need to be working to get a teaching certificate in the first place. You've got parallel universes. You've got the idea that time may not be linear. That all history may be happening at once, we just perceive it as a linear flow. That your thoughts are made up of the same energy forces that make up what we perceive as solid matter, thus you have a hand in shaping your own reality. In other words, prayer really works, which is good news for those of you that didn't study so well for your finals. I see the look on your face. That is the exact same look I want from a student, with that jaw dropped down like that in disbelief. Now I KNOW that I have got their attention. They may not believe a single word that is coming from your mouth, but they will be fascinated by the tall tales that you are spinning. All you need is their interest. *All real learning is emotion based.* With boredom there is no emotion. I remember being a student in a social studies course where I was forced to recognize the difference between a Doric, Corinthian and a host of other columns. Not only did I not care, but I began to loathe entire populations of people - The Romans, the Greeks. I wrote off the whole Mediterranean Sea area as boring. At the start of class, don't begin with mundane details, such as the names of pillars holding up a building. Start with something like nuclear winter. Cloning. Or my personal favorite, light. See this flashlight here. You've got an entire science course here for four ninety-five. You turn it off and on for one second and casually remark, "Oh, by the way, light travels at 69,000 miles per second. If this had been strong enough it would have circled the world and hit me slam in the back of the head. In one second." As an afterthought mention that time is not constant and slows down as it approaches the speed of light. What you are waiting for is for them to call you an opiated liar. That's when you introduce all those facts you want them to learn. They will actually remember them.

How can you tell when you've got their interest? I once showed Ron Howard's excellent science movie about intelligence, determination and heroism, "Appollo 13", to a class full of very challenging students. Even their probation officer said they were challenging. I was afraid this movie was a gamble as far as the "boring" sentiment goes. Towards the end of the movie all you could hear were the kids discussing feverishly their scientific theories on how to provide a safe reentry. The bell rang to go to lunch. Like a fool, I was trying to dismiss them, to finish the movie the next day. "Mr. Johnson, have you lost your mind? People's lives are at stake here. What are you thinking about? We can get ptomaine poisoning anytime." When kids are willing to miss food, they are definitely interested in something!!

In order to get to all those wonderful teachable moments, however, you have to have discipline in the class. Kids are different these days. Many are eaten up with attitude. Don't you just love kids with nasty attitudes? It makes your short life seem so much longer. All of a sudden a day seems like a month. "You can't make me." Now, that's a good one. You're trying to teach the kid how to fill out a check properly and he's going to get all arrogant about it. "You can't make me." It has taken the place of "I'll try harder." Even better is "I don't care." Young man, you just flunked your chemistry test. "I don't care." We have you on video tape destroying the boys bathroom. You'll get three for one on this: "That's not me", then "I didn't do it", followed by "I don't care." I'm calling your parents: that's two for one. "I don't care" and "We don't care." What ever happened to we care - a lot? And even better, we're going to make you care. I'll see you after school. I'll see you on Saturday and bring your work clothes because we are going to have a "we care" fun festival. Whatever happened to that? Oh, yeah. The lawyer thing. "We'll sue." That's a school board member's favorite phrase. You can't do anything anymore without the threat of being sued. If your paperwork isn't right, you can be sued. If you talk to Jimmy too harshly, you can be sued. If Jimmy shoots Johnny because you evidently didn't talk to Jimmy harshly enough, you can be sued. If Sherita can't read, they'll sue you. Or if you retain Sherita, they'll sue you anyway. It doesn't matter what you do, so teachers sit in a paralyzed state of fear while many students bask in their own ignorance and disrespect.

I'm willing to bet my big, fat, teacher's paycheck that same lawyer was given detention at one time, which allowed him to get his mind focused. Allowed him to focus his youthful energy on learning instead of destruction, which allowed him to graduate from law school, which allowed him to make a very nice living off of suing his teachers who got him there in the first place.

What kind of society are we building now? You can't make a child work because that's abuse? That will be news to the vocational instructor. I can see him now as he is locking the door behind him: "Well, until I can figure this out I think I'll go home, slip into my straightjacket, stretch out on my bed and take a little nap."

If truth be told, schools could still do whatever it takes to straighten things out. It's just that lawsuits have turned administrators into an entirely new class of invertebrate. A jelly fish has a stiffer spine. Since they can't control the students anymore they turn their full fury upon the one entity that is more helpless than they are: the teacher. "Mr. Lewis, we have called you to the office because of your inability to control your class. It has come to our attention that Steven has been throwing bourbon bottles in the classroom again and quite frankly, we feel that it is a waste of good liquor and has got to stop." The teacher replied, "I was just wondering, what am I allowed to do?" "You personally, nothing but fill out a bunch of paperwork. But I, as principal, am allowed to get severe and invoke out-of-school suspension." You ever notice how suspension and vacation even sound the same?

And have you ever heard severe and vacation used in the same sentence? Boy, that threat of a vacation is a real behavior controller, isn't it? "Now, if you don't stop setting Suzie's hair on fire I'm going to send you home to an unsupervised setting where you can do anything you want. That'll teach you."

Inability to control the class: the kiss of death for an instructor. It translates into "it's the teacher's fault." Come to think of it, most things translate into "it's the teacher's fault." Kevin's failing, the test scores are low, Shirley was robbed, Pam is pregnant, Frederick is skipping school, Larry can't hold a job, John can't read and Cheryl can't figure out her auto loan. What pops immediately into mind when you hear any of these? "It's the teachers fault." Sure it does.

On the one hand you've got the legislature - the largest body of lawyers outside of the American Bar Association - spending it's time underfunding and misguiding education and then loudly complaining about their own product. On the other hand is another group of lawyers who continuously circle the education system like vultures, waiting to feed off of the mistakes and weaknesses created by the first set of lawyers. Is it just me or is there a connection there? Maybe it is just me, but I swear I see a pattern in there somewhere. At least it leaves teachers off the hook. Don't blame us for any of the school system's problems because we are the only ones who don't have a say in how things are run. It's like blaming the average Iraqi citizen for the way Mr. Hussein was running things. No, no, no. If you bureaucrats want to have all the power, fine. Go ahead and take it. Just take the blame along with it too, please. Take the whole package, thank you very much.

Whatever happened to shame? I'm not talking about the legislature now, I'm talking in the classroom. What's the matter with shame? If it is good enough to be a driving force for a huge chunk of the world, like the entire population of Asia, why is it not good enough for the local school? I remember back in the sixth grade getting together with a couple of buddies and deciding that we weren't going to study for the next Geography test. We made sort of a stupidity pact. Geography was way too hard and besides, we felt that it was irrelevant, anyway. During the Vietnam war, I'm sure that some of those same guys wish that they had been a little more rigorous in their studies. War has a way of making a lot of things more relevant, and in a hurry. Anyway, as it turned out, I was the only one to take our stupidity blood oath seriously. I was the only one to have flunked the test. I found this out while the teacher was reading the test scores OUT LOUD to the class. I was mortified. I was ashamed. I also never did any bonehead thing like that again, and became a fairly good student after that.

I once had a very bright young man in one of my classes who insisted on wearing his pants somewhere down around his knees, exposing his underwear everyday. I had more father-son talks with him than with my entire family. It made no difference. I finally got fed up. During what the Chinese refer to as the Day of the Final Straw, I whipped out a camera that I had bought just for this occasion and took a picture of him in all his purple boxer glory. When the picture spit out of the camera, he watched it develop, agonizingly slow, before his very eyes. He did not wait for it to form a crystal clear picture before he went ballistic. He was so outraged that he wanted to fight me, then and there, in the middle of the class. I thought to myself, this is good. The young man still has a sense of shame, which means self-respect. That I can deal with. It's the guys that would want a framed copy of the photo to send to grandma that I worry about. Shame saved that boy's life, as it did mine. The young man now has a nice job and family and something to laugh about whenever we bump into each other.

The purpose of cultivating a sense of self-respect early in life is to prevent making a big fool out of yourself later in life, when it really matters. It might have prevented what I saw at a SENIOR, and I want to repeat the word SENIOR, science fair. I had entered one side of the gym and was examining a science project when I heard a commotion way at the other side. I started walking that way and saw a bunch of kids standing in a group convulsed with laughter. I mean they were slapping the table and falling on the floor. That type of laughter. Not the kind you particularly want to hear if it is your science project that they are critiquing. I no longer had the slightest bit of interest in the project that I had been looking at, which had been how to get a car to get 400 miles per gallon using common kitchen garbage as a fuel. This other one over there obviously had that one beaten by a country mile. Before I could get there, I noticed a young man rush up - I assumed that he was the humiliated party in all this - and immediately grab his science project, crumple and mangle it the best he could while running full tilt for the exit. Now, I worry about our future scientists. I don't think that they are as curious as the students of yesteryear. The ones that hadn't seen the project actually let that young man disappear with a shrug. I AM a student from yesteryear, however, and had to know. I found his project in the trash and took it home, where it still sits in a place of honor. This young man had evidently assumed, like a lot of kids, that a deadline was not a deadline. That the future is some abstract thing that never morphs into the present. Either that, or he was taking massive amounts of drugs that mess with short term memory. Anyway, he had obviously done his project approximately ten minutes before it was due, in the wild hopes of getting a "D" minus, minus, instead of an "F". He had gotten himself three pieces of poster board and lashed them together with scotch tape and stood them up on the table. On the left one, he had written "Glasses are very, very important." On the middle one, he had taped a pair of beat- up eyeglasses that he got from who knows where, and on the right one he wrote "They come from far, far away." The whole thing was almost Zen-like. It was simple, yet deep at the same time. The long and the short of all this, is that I am not sure that the emphasis in education these days on protecting kids self esteem at all costs is going to produce the type of adult that we need in society. A young man should not be fleeing for his sanity in high school. That should happen in elementary school, while you have plenty of time to recover from the emotional scars. That way, by the time you're in high school, you'll act like it. You'd be too ashamed not to.

I wonder what that young man's parents would have thought about all this. Mostly, I just wonder about what parents are thinking about, period. I mean, what's up with parents these days? Not the good ones, of which there are plenty, thank God, but the swelling army of parents that live in La-La Land. I would like to know the exact date that teachers became the enemy? I would like to mark it on my calendar to remember, because I never got the bulletin about it. They probably slipped it in by e-mail, which I evidently ignore at my own peril. It used to be that you looked forward to seeing parents at a parent - teacher meeting. They were there to see how Laura was doing and what they could do at the house to help facilitate her education. Now it's called a parent - teacher inquisition and you find yourself sitting at the wrong side of the table asking yourself two questions: Is that a microphone over there, and why is it pointed at me? And you are now answering what has become the parental mantra these days, "what did you do to my child?" Not "for", but "to" my child.

Now, I know why this change in climate has come about. Somewhere up the ladder there is an elected official in charge of the school system. And, God bless them, they aren't real good at handling pressure. They would last approximately thirty seconds in your average middle school. Angry parents are hurricane force pressure, which will blow a tinker toy house down every time. I don't blame them. It's just the nature of the beast. They just shouldn't have anything to say about the day- to -day operation of a school. That used to be why they hired principals. So, I can see why the teacher is on the hot seat. I have a little more problem with the thought process of the angry parent, because their anger comes from the fact that they actually believe every single thing that their child tells them. EVERY thing. "The teacher asked me to sit down and I wouldn't so he started to threaten me and I think he had a knife in his pocket and he cursed me in class and threw me to the ground and I had to defend myself so I punched him in the head and ran out of the room." The normal parent of the past would have calmly stopped the conversation right after "the teacher asked me to sit down, but I wouldn't." The only thing that would have been heard after that would be a gurgling and whimpering sound coming from the choke hold. A lot of today's parents are actually going to back their child up, no matter WHAT they have done. They will believe them and they will back them, at all costs to reality. True story: There was a young man who decided to take a short cut to success by robbing a car in the parking lot of an apartment complex. The problem was, he wasn't very good at it. A little on the noisy side. The owner of the car heard something and came out onto his second story balcony to see what was going on. He shouted at the young man to get away from his car. The young man, thinking that a gun was going to make him "bad", whipped one out and pointed it at the car owner. What it really makes you is a target, however, and the car owner shot at him several times. The mom's reaction was anger at the car owner. "He didn't have to shoot at my son with a gun." Oh? Well, maybe the grenade launcher wasn't handy. Maybe he had foolishly left it out in the garage.

You know, denial is a nice place to visit if it's the river you're talking about. But don't live there if it's not. Sometimes your kid is just plain wrong. It doesn't mean that you don't love them. Just don't be stupid about it. I had a parent get furious one time because her son had gone home and told her that I had stolen his shirt. I explained to her that I had taken the shirt because it had gang graffiti all over it, assuming that she would be glad to get the heads up. I found myself lost in the twilight zone arguing over whether or not the "Killer East Side Boyz" was a gang or just a club. I told her that if any of the club members are holding their meetings at midnight outside of apartment complexes that they may want to up their dues to pay for the health insurance. But she was just doing what all good parents do: protecting her child from thieving teachers. You know, if parents and teachers went back to being allies, maybe there would be fewer young men performing feats of desperation in dark parking lots. And better dressed, to boot.

It all comes down to respect. There is a diminishing respect for anything in society these days. Our kids are eaten up with disrespect, which is a problem, because you can't teach a single thing to someone who disrespects you. So, before you even pick up your dry erase marker, you need to have a respect discussion with yourself, because respect is not coming from the outside these days, so it better be found someplace deep down in. Are you a teacher with a little "t" or capital "T"? If you are dealing with a self view in the lower case, do yourself a favor and use your teaching certificate to start a marshmallow roast because at least it would have served a purpose, if only for a short period of time. I once had a student who, on being asked to pick up the trash that she had thrown down, spit out, "I don't have to do that. You're not the principal!" We locked eyes and I replied, "No, I'm not. I am a teacher." It took a couple of minutes for it to sink in that my view of teacher was a lot more Zeus-like than hers, and she picked up the trash. The "teacher stare", when done right, is a wonderful thing to behold. If you wear glasses like I do, you cock your head downward just a little and look over the top of them, wearing what General Patton would call his "war face". It's great. It has the Medusa effect.

    A teacher called me one day from his class, very depressed. His class was totally out of control. He asked me to come to his room. When I got there I pulled him aside and asked, "How much power do you think teachers have these days?" He shook his head. "Not much, I'm afraid." I whispered to him, "You have as much power as you think you have." He looked startled. I then turned on the class like Gulliver in Lilliput. "So, you all are in training to be nurses, are you? I wouldn't let you take my temperature. I might end up dead. Any of you that want out of this program sign this sheet of paper and get your momma on the phone. We will make it official. Everybody else, please sit down." "But Mr. Johnson, this stuff is boring." "That's fine. Get your mother on the phone. She needs to know why Mrs. Smith died in your care: because you thought platelettes were boring. There's the phone."

Part of the trick is to let them think that you are insane; that you will go to ANY lengths to get them a proper education. I cultivate this insanity thing. I once had a student go on a cursing spree in class, on top of refusing to do any work. I calmly told him I was putting an "F" for the day in the grade book. Of course, he couldn't care less. I then gave him an "F" in the next box, for the next day. Now I had his attention. "You can't do that!" You notice how they know right from wrong when it comes to YOUR behavior. "I repeat, are you going to do your work?" "Hell, no!" I put an "F" in the next box. "Wait! I said you can't do that!" I put an "F" in the next box. "I'm going to bring my dad to school." "Please do. And your mom, Aunt Suzie, Uncle Fred, and anybody else who cares to listen to why I had to fill in all those boxes to keep you from destroying yourself and this class. I want to see them tomorrow." I now had a reasonable human being on my hands. My personal attention getter is to threaten to eat dinner at their house. And then make it happen. You will never again have trouble with a surly young man after you have had dinner with the family. You will probably not have much trouble from ANYBODY in the class after that. The fact that you can show up at the dinner table is a shot across the bow that the entire crew will notice. And your insanity reputation will reach legendary proportions, which is what you want. Another trick is to call home, during class, when everybody can hear you. "Yes, she's doing excellent work today, you can be very proud of her. She is one of the finest young ladies I have ever met. I'm sure that she will go far in life. She has the skills be a success at whatever she puts her mind to. It is nothing but a pleasure to have her in my class. Have a blessed day." Click. Insanity takes many forms. The entire class is thinking, "If he's crazy enough to make a call like that out of the blue, well, maybe he'll do that for me." And they're right. I am just that crazy.

There is no greater power than positive words spoken about one's child. A well functioning family unit is crucial for a child's success later in life. If the teacher becomes part of that family unit, it doubles in strength in its ability to create a successful child. How does one become part of a family? Just care deeply for a parent's child, that's all. If they sense that from you, they will happily dump worthless Uncle John out of his seat and offer it to you.

You have to do things that aren't quite ordinary to prove your credentials, however. They're not going to give you Uncle John's seat for nothing. I had a student come up to me and whisper in my ear, "Mr. Johnson, Martha is not sick, she's skipping class today." "I see. Where is she at?" "Probably at the drug store. She likes to shop." She meant shoplift, but I got the message. I got another teacher to hold my class and snuck into the store without Martha seeing me. I planted myself in the middle of the beauty aide aisle and waited for her to come around the corner. The look on her face when she saw me was worth the ride up there. It probably would have been worth the ride to Quebec. After I called mom I delivered Martha to her doorstep. I was now an official family member. Mom knew that it could just as easily have been a police car informing her of her daughters arrest or her being found in the trunk of some psycho's car. Nothing puts the fear into a parent more than a fourteen year old girl who thinks she's grown. Martha never skipped class again and is holding down a very nice job as we speak. My job got a lot easier after that, too. I was elected by the student's to the crazy hall of fame. I could tell, because they would say things like, "You better listen to that man. He's liable to do anything." Which is a good thing. The more omniscient they perceive you, the better. You don't ever want a child to perceive you as their equal. If they do they will spend all of their energy locked in a power struggle instead of learning anything useful.

And Lord knows that kids have a lot of energy. You could power your average suburban neighborhood for an entire year with the energy expended by kids in a small middle school. That is why you have to be in charge of your classroom. If you are arguing with the Energizer Bunny all day, guess who is going to wear out first? When it comes down to it, you are in a sense not a teacher at all, but a power plant technician. It is your job to harness and direct this powerful flow of energy in the right direction, which would be education instead of destruction. You will find yourself saying, "You know, if that student would put his mind on his studies instead of foolishness, he could be Albert Einstein." You will find yourself saying that a lot. I had a young man once who was constantly hatching get rich schemes that ranged anywhere from misdemeanors to felonies. I was working at a vocational school at the time and, try as I might, could not find any of his plans in my curriculum guide. I called him up to my desk after overhearing that his plots were now including bodily harm, and sat him down. "Julio, I have been studying your talents for a long time and am convinced of a way that you can make $30,000. In one year. Seriously." His ears flattened back like a race horse as he pulled his face close to mine. "How, Mr. Johnson? Is it safe? I mean selling drugs is getting scary out there. The streets are full of crazy people." "It has nothing to do with drugs." "Oh. Well, prostitution is not as easy as it looks. You know that those women actually hate men. And don't make one of them mad, because they're already mad enough anyway." "No," I said, "it doesn't have anything to do with prostitution. Lean forward a little more and I'll tell you... GET A JOB!" You could hear the entire class roar. What makes this funny and sad is that the answer caught him completely by surprise.

The poster child for misplaced brilliance came from a young man that I had when I was the behavioral specialist at a facility for children expelled from the regular school system. There were certain rules to be regularly followed so that they could eventually function properly in a less strict setting. One of them was a dress code. Horror of horrors, you had to wear your shirt tucked into your pants, which were to be worn at the waist, anchored there by a belt.

By the response, Alcatraz has a much looser dress code. One morning, what the students affectionately called the prison bus, pulled up to the school. And off steps Kelvin in all his glory. The director turned away to keep from laughing. All I could say is, "Oh, no, he didn't." This young man had probably spent the better part of a week figuring out how to do right and wrong at the exact same time. More precisely, how to do wrong, and you know it's wrong, but get away with it because it's in the thin disguise of doing right. I shudder to think about the future if Kelvin takes up politics. He had somehow talked his grandmother into removing his belt loops from the outside of his pants and sew them to the inside of his pants, so that he could wear them inside out and still meet the dress code: pants pulled up at the waist, shirt tucked in. Except that his pockets were sticking straight out in every direction. I greeted him at the bus. "Kelvin, you're the man. You are a stone cold genius. Now, I'm going to give you fifteen minutes to strut around and be the man, then you're going to have to get dressed properly." Kelvin, of course, went into full tilt lawyer mode, which is when the director came up and changed fifteen minutes to fifteen seconds.

Grandmothers, God bless them, shouldn't be put in the position of raising teenagers. Some are good at it, but many are so full of love for the child, that they are clueless. They just want to make little Jimmy happy. "Yes, I sewed those palm tree leaves on your shirts for you. I didn't realize that palm trees were so big among teenagers." Now the kid is wearing four ounces of marijuana on his shirt to school. You know, there shouldn't be a steroid scandal in the U.S. They're just giving it to the wrong people. Medicare should offer a steady supply to Grandmothers everywhere. And a booklet on how to be suspicious of ANYTHING. "What do you mean you want a snowman t-shirt? It's the middle of July. And you're 19 tears old. And don't think I don't know what snowman stands for. Your nose has been running like Niagra falls. What's next? A Santa Clause shirt? What does Santa stand for? Murder? You kids have no respect for nothing. Teddy Bear mean heroin? Don't ask me for snow nothing-snowflake, snowboard, snowstorm. Nothing. And what's up with your hair? It looks like your head exploded. Go back to that bathroom and don't come out until you look like Denzel. Don't you dare look at me like that. Grandma's gone right wing and joined the NRA. And while you're in there, tuck your shirt in!" Grandmas on steroids. A teacher's best friend.

America is so different these days. The family unit itself is under siege from so many different directions, that I worry about our children's future. It is, after all, the bulwark of our democracy, our very civilization. Who is there to step in and fill the gap? Who is society going to lean on more and more to prop up civilization? I'll tell you who. YOU. Teachers. Schools. You will be underpaid, disrespected, overworked, ignored, and undervalued. But when push comes to shove it is you that they will turn to, to save this whole country. You are the Winston Churchill of professions.

Children do not raise themselves very well.

Somebody has got to do it. It's not as if children would live in a state of peaceful tranquility and co-existence if left to their own devices. In reality it's a "Lord of the Flies" world out there. Let's get Piggy. Remember how sweet your classmates were to anybody that deviated from the norm. I think that soldiers in Stalingrad had more fun than an alienated teenager. I remember my first year in high school. I had glasses, wore nice pants with cuffs and road a bicycle to school. On top of this my parents thought that carrying a briefcase to school would make me look educated. I got an education all right.

So if there are way too few functioning households, and the public school system is under siege, what have we got? We have YOU. You run your class the best you can. You stand firm when others don't. You care for your students when others won't. And God will bless you for it. And if you're lucky, and you hang in long enough, somebody, somewhere, is going to come back and say "thank you." And, quite frankly, it doesn't get any better than that.

It has been my privilege to have been here tonight. Have a great night and even better career. Thank you.

Preface

"So, You STILL Want To Be A teacher?" was a lecture given to teachers in the Crandall County School System in southwest Georgia, 2004.

SO, YOU STILL WANT TO BE A TEACHER?

What a beautiful day here in Georgia. I went and visited one of your schools yesterday and while I was in the cafeteria I saw something very disturbing. Over by the cash register I noticed some commotion going on. It appeared that someone was haggling with the food manager about the price of the meal. I thought to myself, it is a shame that here, in the United States of America, a child could come from a background so destitute that a dollar seventy-five for a full, three course meal seems unreasonable. So, I walked over to see if I could lend some assistance. Once I got there everything became clear. That was no child; that was a young teacher. Who else would be arguing so vehemently for something under five dollars? What was disturbing to me was the thought that whatever college this young lady came from did a lousy job of preparing her for this profession. I mean, she actually thought that she was going to make real money ? What do they teach people these days? Now, if you are in this room and think teaching is a get rich quick scheme you need to go back to your university and get your money back. And take some economics courses while you are at it. It's not even a get rich slow scheme. You better have a higher sense of purpose than money to be in the classroom, otherwise you won't last. It can be the most draining job in the world. People envy your vacation time, because it allows you a chance to have a real life, which is alien in this dog-eat-dog world we are fast developing. It's not vacation, it's recovery time. It's even hard to enjoy the vacation, because every time you look at the calendar, it is getting closer to NOT being vacation. You can tell how underpaid teachers are when so many sign up to teach summer school. That's like a veteran stumbling out of Guadicanal, going home and the first thing he does is reenlist, because he needs bucks for an oil change for the car.

You definitely need a higher sense of purpose to stay in the classroom for those children, year after year. Because if you are not there, who is going to be? When you look over your sea of faces in the morning, many of those looking back at you are staring at the only real adult in their life, especially in schools anchored in communities that are struggling. That thought alone should put some starch in your spine. To achieve my higher sense of purpose, I wanted to empower myself as much as possible. In order to do this I would take on extra-curricular duties ON PURPOSE. It was either empowering or a sign of creeping dementia, I can't remember which. Oh, yeah, you thought that because of the low pay that you only had to work from eight to three-thirty. Oh, no, you're expected to perform *duties*. If they called it volunteers, nobody would show. You learn a lot from duties, however.

I was at the door of the gym one night, selling tickets to a basketball game. The tickets were a whole dollar. The game was halfway over when this young man walked up and started hassling me about the price of admission. He wanted to pay fifty cents since it was halftime. I explained that the program needed the money and, besides, what's the big deal over a dollar anyway? He was steady crying over the blatant unfairness of it all. This went on for what seemed like forever when he finally relented. He proceeded to pull a wad of fifties and twenties out of his pocket that I estimated to be three inches thick. To show that his wad of drug money made him a much bigger man than teachers, who foolishly slave for a living, he ever so slowly thumbed through his riches until he came across a lowly one dollar bill. Now, I like a challenge as well as the next man. "Excuse me, you must have misunderstood, the tickets are forty dollars." "WHAT?" "You heard me." "But I've got to get in there. My Grandma and my girlfriend are already in there waiting on me." "Yes, I know." The power had now shifted back to where it was supposed to be. He learned a lesson and the school got some badly needed funds.

Kids are funny. It's never really about money, it's about power. I have been on guard duty at the back gate of a football stadium and seen kids scale a barbed wire fence to save a buck. Now, it's beneath their dignity to bend over and pick up a dime but they are willing to rip their leg off for ten of them. This is obviously not about dimes. These young men had a power point to prove.

The use of power is a funny thing. The acceptance of rules all depends on the perception of where that power is coming from. Nobody likes the use of arbitrary power, especially teenagers. That's why you will hear the battle cry "It's not fair!" whenever you are arguing with a child. Kids need to know that you CARE for them. That's all. If you establish that early, then your use of power is not perceived as arbitrary, but purpose driven. Now you can discipline all you want to. I was at the same back gate one night when a bevy of drunks showed up. They were about two feet from me on the other side of the fence and were having what appeared to be a profanity contest. I asked them to tone it down a little but they had "you're not going to tell me what to do" written all over their faces. I got a lesson in life that night. When one of them snarled "WHY?" at me I replied, "Look through the gate here. There are women and children in there." This he understood and the transformation was instantaneous. He turned to his friends and told them to shut up. "Can't you see there are women and children in there? Show some respect." For the next hour we had a pleasant but somewhat incoherent conversation through the gate.

The cafeteria duty post is another great place for life lessons. I was in the cafeteria at the vocational school where I worked, training exceptional education students for jobs, when I saw a young man throw his trash from his table onto the floor. When asked to pick it up, I was informed that " this is what janitors are for." A friend of his picked the paper up and placed it on the table, as if to make the situation all right. I replaced the trash to the floor, because there was only one person in the room that could make the situation all right, and it wasn't the surly gentleman's polite friend. *A little teacher advice here. Don't ever pick a fight that you are not going to win. Don't ever make a request of a child, no matter how small, that you don't have a game plan to enforce.* If you ever can't enforce it, you are no longer a teacher, but a beggar with a fancy sheet of paper on the wall. At least beggars are good at wheedling money out of people, which is something that union representatives need to brush up on. Anyway, I informed this student that he was being trained for a sixty thousand dollar a year job and that I didn't expect this ridiculous behavior from a professional-to-be. This was all news to him, of course, because the average teenager's view of the future is whether or not to go to the mall on Friday night. My particular game plan worked like a charm because I could see the principal coming up the walkway to the cafeteria and knew in advance that the boy was doomed. He ended up cleaning up the cafeteria for a week, under the direction of the now-respected janitor. Fast forward six months. I am in the middle of giving my "no thank you, no food" sermon while at the same time pointing to young men's heads, the universal signal for "please remove your hat or it's mine" when this same young man approached me. He looked me straight in the eye and said, "Mr. Johnson, why are you the only one who loves us?" "What in the world are you talking about?" "You're on us constantly, like a chicken on a Junebug. You act as if you actually expect us to be somebody." I paused for a second. "That is exactly what I expect. Don't you have a business exam coming up? Well, what are you doing standing here talking to me for? Go study." Off he went. I figured it wasn't going to do anybody any good to see a grown man weeping openly in the cafeteria. It might cast suspicion on the food. Discipline is not authority for authority's sake. That is fascism. I mean, exactly how high did your blood pressure go the last time you got a ticket for going fifty-six in a fifty-five mile per hour speed zone? *Discipline for purpose. Everything good that comes from it stems from that higher place that you are coming from.*

Aah, but authority used properly is a beautiful thing to behold. I was teaching at a vocational school when we heard that we were going to get a new principal. There was nothing wrong with the old principal. As a matter of fact, he was doing a great job, so they rewarded him by shipping him out to Siberia. Ever notice that? Don't ever get attached to somebody competent. "Where'd John go? He was right over there just a minute ago." It happens so quick you could snap your neck looking for him. You might not want to get too competent your own self. Anyway, we were getting a new principal. According to the rumor mill she was reviled on Earth and four other planets. I have learned to wait to pass judgement, however; you will learn that as you go mostly by listening to the vicious rumors being told about yourself. Most teachers read bulletins but some get their news from the hate monger in the class down the hall. So, I am waiting to see. During her third day there I am doing parking lot duty after school. The buses are lined up, followed by a row of cars. One of the students got impatient, gunned his car around the buses and blew past me, ignoring my yelling. He could not ignore the new principal, however, who stepped out into the parking lot in front of his car, laying her hand on the hood as he came to a screeching stop. She proceeded to yank the keys out of the ignition, informed him that if he ever tried that stunt again she would get his license revoked and that he was to drive slowly back to the end of the line and wait until every man, woman, and child had left campus. She handed him back his keys. Mr. Meek did what he was told, with a "Yes, ma'am" thrown in for good measure. This was my reaction. "Ma'am, are you married? Because if not, I'd like to talk with you. You can wear your drill instructor's uniform at the alter if you want to. I love uniforms." Now I know what soldiers felt like when they saw Joan of Arc doing her thing for the first time. I would have walked through fire for that woman. I was used to principals who viewed student misbehavior as something wrong with the teacher. They'd say things like, "Oh, come now, he doesn't look that drunk to me. What's the problem here?" Personally, I cannot stand wishy-washy authority figures. They are an invitation to disaster. If you are on night recon patrol and the enemy is somewhere up ahead, what you don't want to see is the lieutenant looking dazed, confused, afraid, or any combination of the three.

What I do wish, though, is that whenever a teacher does work their way up the system into positions of authority that they would stop pretending that they've got Alzheimer's. Ever notice that? They forget totally what it was like in the classroom. "What do you mean forty-eight kids in a math class is too many? You're a whiner, aren't you? Well, you can thank your lucky stars that you even have a job. Not too many jobs for whiners out there." And this is after only four days of being in administration. What happens? Do they perform science experiments on people in the central office, or what? I've always thought how much fun it would be to be superintendent. The gags you could pull. "William, I've just been informed that your position has been cut. You will have to go back to the classroom." The administrator's hanging all onto your leg as you're trying to walk away, weeping all over your pants cuff, wailing like he's being sent to the lower rung of Hades. "Just kidding, William. Come on, get up and pull yourself together." See, it's proof that the Alzheimer thing is fake. They remember, all right.

Speaking of wailing and moaning, I believe I mentioned that I taught exceptional education for a long time. I don't know how to break this to anybody, but teaching by ditto sheet doesn't exactly prepare your students for the real world, unless they are planning on moving to Ditto Land, and staying there forever. During English class I would have my students write a page per day, minimum. Well, this was an outrage. The hand wringing and pleading were almost comical. After being informed that they could work on whatever, including raps, they were somewhat mollified. Then they were told that the only rules were that they could not curse or use the "N" word. Now the hand wringing really began. "Oh, so we can't write about anything?" "What do I say now?" In their mind I had stolen their entire means of expression. They were literally helpless.

To a teenage male this thug-life thing is the

greatest invention since french fries, not realizing that both can kill you. It's a modern day version of Tom Sawyer fantasizing about being a pirate. You get to disrespect, steal, kill, abuse women, be rich, free, violent, and abuse women. And get away with it. It's a great lifestyle that these kids aspire to. Thug life has rotted the brains clear out of their head. They have collectively lost their minds. "Alright Kelvin, we are going to write in debate format today. Pick which side you want to defend." "I can't do that. I've got to rap." "Why is that?" "Because I'm a ghetto man." "You're not a ghetto man." Now he's getting testy: "I AM a ghetto man." "Kelvin, I can see your house from here. It's the nicest two story on the block." And this is the white kid. God only knows how deeply embedded this self-image is in the other kids. "Johnny, you're not a thug. You have to learn this math. Don't hand me that. I don't care if you ARE going to be a crack dealer, this math will help." They are bombarded with so many negative images these days. They are being programmed from birth to view themselves in a negative light. Let me stress that this is not a black thing. This is a male teenage stupidity thing. A rainbow coalition of misdirected lifestyle.

  Since I took the "N" word from them, some of the black kids were at a total loss as to how to describe themselves. My suggestions, being positive, were seen as totally worthless. I had a student come up, paper in hand, who had been trying to work his way out of this dilemma. "Mr. Johnson, can I use figger?" "No, the word is figure." Then he showed me his paper and I realized that all he wanted was an "N" word rhyming substitute. I looked at him. "Now you've finally done it. You snuck out of your house last night and joined the Klan." "But I didn't use the word." "I didn't even realize that black guys were eligible for membership. That's O.K. with me, though. That pointy head of yours will probably fit nicely into that pointy little hat they gave you. Why don't you sit down and practice respecting yourself!"

One other time I told a student to get his mother on the phone and call her that to her face. If it was O.K. with her, it was O.K. with me. He declined. Once that gentleman sat down, here comes a white student, paper in hand. No "N" word problem here. He just wants to write about Satan. For the hundred and fifth time. At least he's never late to school. It's probably because he only spends two seconds on picking out his wardrobe in the morning, because every single stitch of clothing he wears is jet-black. I don't know where he got it from, but he even has matching dental floss.

I don't understand this Goth deal. Some of the white kids are a tough nut to crack. They just want to be dead. They even come to school dressed for the funeral. They just don't get the "life is basically good" concept. They will look at you with a combination of contempt and pity if you try to press the point. "Poor, deluded, Mr. Johnson. Doesn't he know that every second of existence stinks?" I could see if he was just talking about school here, but he's talking about the whole ball of wax. A few students get a little carried away. They'd wear a hockey mask to school if it wasn't against the dress code.

A lot of kids have turned complaining about life into an art form. I don't really care as long as it is done on paper, using correct grammar. The heck with a teacher's aide. What every classroom really needs is a school psychologist. Preferably two.

All kids should learn how to write. It is evidently very cathartic. I love the Hispanic kid in the back. No agenda, he just wants to learn how to spell properly.

I realize that these kids are just modeling what they are surrounded with, so I combat models with models. "Ever hear of this rapper?", I'd ask them. "His name is Langston Hughes." They loved his stuff. Now they could raise their writing from just idiotic rhyming - what I lovingly call, "Rhyme, dime, crime"whenever I'm asked my opinion - to rhyming about something; ideas that were purposeful. Some of their stuff approached art. Only later did they find out that Langston Hughes was a poet and by then it was too late.

While I'm on this modeling idea, I sometimes wonder what some parents are thinking about. Most parents are way cool but there are a few that just take your breath away. I mean, isn't there some kind of test that you have to pass before you get to take your baby out of the hospital? They do it for drivers licenses. One day Mrs. Franklin was called to the school to pick up her son, who was out of control. She drove up to the school in a fury. Furious at the school, of course, not her son. She parks the car in front of a classroom, music blaring from the car, and gets out to go find junior. I guess that a guy shrieking profanities like a drunken sailor on his first shore leave is music. At least it's sold as music. It didn't seem to phase the baby sitting in the car seat, but it sure gave Mrs. Lawson's class something to talk about for the next month.

One time I had a student's uncle curse me out over the phone. In this modern era of child rearing there often is no parent so it falls on one of the relatives to yell at the teacher. He was so drunk that he couldn't even curse me properly. I had to help him with the words.

And then there are the clueless. "I don't know what is the matter with my son. He's always getting into trouble. I don't know where he gets all these crazy ideas. Oh, look at the time. I've got to hurry home. It's our family movie night. Tonight is a classic: "The Endless Torture of Innocent Little Jimmy." It's probably on a double feature with "You Stole My Head and I Want it Back."

I must admit, parents don't get a lot of help from Mr. Big Business these days. The dolls made for kids all look like a bunch of little strippers. I don't know if this is doing anything to a girl's self image, but I did notice a very happy boy walk out of Toys R Us with a dozen of them. Maybe it does have an effect, because baton twirling has been replaced by pole dancing at many high school football games. You can't even go to the local video store anymore. To get to the family movies you have to wade through the horror section. By the time you get to "Bow Wow the Wonder Dog" the child has been traumatized speechless by the covers showing people with nails sticking out of their head. The heck with parents, what is ANYBODY thinking about these days? I have a radical teacher idea. I don't think that sacrificing our children so that some greed head can make a dollar is a real good idea.

We have to realize that some children have parents by biology only, so the schools have to fill the parent-vacuum void. That's why it kills me that there's all this money for technology and yet teacher's salaries are a disgrace, class sizes are swelling, and there is no money in the budget for real, live human beings, not even paraprofessionals, who are only paid five dollars a day, anyway. Struggling kids from broken homes don't need another piece of machinery. They don't need a Game Boy, they need a GROWN MAN, who is there when they need them. Father Flanagan saved countless boys from ruin at Boys Town. He didn't have technology. He could barely scrape up money to keep the phone working.

Many students could really use some counselors to talk things through, but there aren't any. Oh, they're still called counselors but they don't have time to actually counsel anybody. They are test administrators and paper pushers now but they won't call them that because nobody in their right mind would spend four years of their lives in college if they thought that this is how it was going to end up.

Since there are way too few adults in the school system, how do those that choose to remain deal with the litany of problems that they face everyday? Some how, some way, you need to develop a belief system; in yourself, in your children. One day I was driving down this beautiful back road when I came upon a sign that read "Linclon's Birthplace-12 miles" which pointed off to the left. I was curious, so I detoured. You cannot realize the brutal poverty in which he was raised, by illiterate parents, until you stare and touch - which you are not supposed to do, by the way - this miserable little chicken coop in which he was born. The emotional hurricane that this touched off inside of me forced me to retreat to my car where I could fall apart in private. I don't want to hear one word about what a student can't do. I don't want to hear nothing from nobody about what a child can't do. Anybody can be anything. I know, because I HAVE SEEN IT. It is real to me. It needs to be real to you before you walk into that classroom. There is a little town called Greenville near Tallahassee, FL. where there is an incredible statue of Ray Charles sitting in a little park. If you ever get there, go hug the statue. If you don't believe in the impossible, go hug that statue. Go somewhere, do something to give yourself an epiphany. "Anybody can be anything" is a double barreled belief system, because it applies to yourself as well as your children and it may be the one thing that keeps you in the classroom instead of lighting out for the nearest psychiatrist when things get rough, which often happens before your second cup of coffee. Besides, you can't afford a psychiatrist anyway, unless you think that you can vent your frustrations in under three minutes.

    It may just be the immaturity of the brain, but a good psychiatrist may be useful in explaining how a child's view of reality and a teacher's view of reality are often two very different things. You can catch a child, hammer in hand, in the middle of a sea of broken TV's and VCR's and their reaction is, "You're picking on me." I had a student come running up to me once, yelling that Brad had thrown my car keys onto the gym roof. When I saw Brad and asked him why he had done that he replied, "Because I found them and didn't know who they belonged to." This is what passes for logic.

Or sometimes their view of reality is different because they are higher than a Chinese box kite. What I love is when kids come into the classroom high and think you won't notice. I had a young man once who was standing on his desk in the middle of class playing his air guitar. He seemed genuinely depressed when I pointed out that he was in class and not on stage. I had him touch and name some school - type objects to ground him back on earth, such as "globe", "wall", and "letter to parent."

I had another young man who had been having trouble with fractions and measurements. I figured that I would throw him a softball so that he could gain some confidence, so I asked him how many inches there were in a foot. I should have asked him something easier, like was that a half or three quarters of a joint that you smoked before class, because he stared at me with a look of horror before he blurted out, "That's a trick question, Mr. Johnson's trying to trick me" and began running around the room, searching for his sanity I presumed. I talked to him and his father later. I've got news for you, ANY question you ask Cheech and Chong is a trick question. Marijuana and the classroom don't mix well. The short term memory loss thing is a definite problem. You're trying to chastize a student that you've had for a year and they're stammering, "Now, don't tell me, I'll get it. Who are you again?"

Then there are the students who try to kill school boredom by doing cocaine. Now, there's a brilliant move. "Young lady, could you sit still for a second, you're driving everyone nuts in here?" "I can't." "Well, could you please stop chewing on your blouse? It's very distracting." They've got the crazed look on their face that a claustrophobic sailor has who's been in the submarine a little too long. "Lucy, would you like to run an errand for me?" "Oh, YES. Yes, I would." "Here you go. And I do mean run."

Alcohol is another great one for the classroom. You hear yelling coming from the back of the class. "What are you looking at? You want to fight?" "Larry, you're picking on the statue of Beethoven."

Don't be dismayed. These are what are referred to as teachable moments. Kids are desperate for knowledge. They are thirsting to learn, it's just that they never seem to want to learn what you are teaching at that particular time. So, to heck with the curriculum, go with the moment. It's easy. Let's take chemistry. Everything is made up of atoms and atoms clumped together are called molecules. Oxygen is O_2. Alcohol is OH. Notice that there is only one O in alcohol, instead of the two needed to sustain life. So that if you chug-a-lug like some nut that you see in the movies, you are in serious danger of asphyxiating yourself. You have now taught more in one minute than in the previous six weeks combined because you have the two elements that kids crave: interest and drama. Kids live for drama. Their whole life is one big drama. Listen to a group of teenage girls sometime. From a distance you can see how agitated and animated they are, so you rush forward to see if you can help. When you get there it turns out that one of the young lady's nail polish was the wrong shade for her dress.

Let's take math. Loretta is in the back. "I'm bored. I wish I was shopping." "Alright, Loretta, let's go shopping. We'll even take our friend, Mr. Credit Card." Squeals of delight emanate from the class. "Let's buy that beautiful prom dress that you've been drooling over. Let's spend one hundred dollars." More squeals of delight. "Now, what is 18% of one hundred? You remember per cent. Cent means one hundredth. Let's see now, that comes to an extra eighteen dollars. What do you mean "WHAT?" And if you pay the minimum payments each month, well, will you look at that? If you stretch it out long enough, you've got yourself a hundred dollar prom dress for only three hundred and fifty dollars. What do you mean is that legal?" This is great. You've got them asking perfectly intelligent questions about not only economics, but the law.

Now that you have their attention you have to get their respect. Respect is a funny thing. To a teacher it should be given automatically, but often is not. If you overhear a child cursing her own mother on her cell phone because she can't borrow the car that night-some nonsense about Aunt Ginny having to go to the hospital-then you know that the respect war will be coming to the classroom. The home front has already been leveled and lost.

You often have to earn respect. You cannot teach without it, however. In Asia they call it face. Saving face and losing face are two very real dynamics in Asian culture. Unfortunately, in some American school systems where all the power is held in just one or two hands on campus, teachers are set up to lose face on an hourly basis. This is why in many classes teachers spend at least half their time on trying to maintain discipline; trying to figure out who is the teacher in the room. Another teacher friend of mine likes to joke about the joys of teaching in Japan. Salaries are double what we make. You only teach for half a day, the other half being spent with your colleagues going over what works and what doesn't. You walk through the grocery store with your chest puffed out because you are not just respected, but revered. Even more than doctors. The professor greets his student at the door with the thwack of a bamboo cane, the student thanks him for getting his mind right and has a seat, eager for work. We fantasized about teaching in Japan a lot.

So one day on courtyard duty I was lost in my fantasy world when I heard "Hey, boy. Hey John Boy!" Realizing I'm not in Japan anymore I looked around at the hundreds of students to find the gentleman who has made me his pet project for the day. I saw him hiding behind a building, peeping out and yelling, "Hey, John Boy!" again, in case any of the other four hundred students hadn't heard his bellowing the first time. Now it's face saving time. I had no idea who the young man was, so I started my respect journey by going to the administration, or what could be referred to in some schools as the Department of Face Losing. I was told by the administration to ignore it. John Boy was a good name. He was just calling me that because he liked me, even if the emphasis was on "boy". I'm now dealing with a person who thinks that this young man with the drop pants and toothpick in his mouth goes home after school and watches reruns of "The Waltons."

Now, as any African American in this country can tell you, it is not an overly good idea to let people stand around and call you "boy" when you are not one. It becomes habit forming amongst those who are inclined to extreme disrespect, and doesn't do much for your own self-respect either. To make a long story short, it took me three days to find out who the young man was. It took a stern, face-to-face talking to, another one between principal, student and myself, and one more between parent and myself before I got respect from him. I knew I had it when one day there was a knock on my door and there was Robert standing there. He said, "Mr. Johnson, if you've got time I could use your help. I don't understand Algebra and I'm flunking." This was a regular - ed student coming to the door of a special - ed teacher, in public and broad daylight no less, to ask for help.

To you who are aspiring to become exceptional-ed teachers, you've got a double fight for respect because the students you are teaching are considered losers and, therefore, you are the loser teacher. So you've got to raise yourself from loser teacher to teacher with a small "t" and then to teacher with a capital "T".

I once had a student who was sent to me from a school for students with severe emotional problems. I was at a vocational school so I was not only educating him but training him for a job. It was an experiment that I felt was worth trying. He had been doing fairly well off and on but one day lost it completely in class: arguing, screaming, knocking things over and threatening to kick my posterior. I reminded him of the game plan in case of this type of outburst which was that I would call security from his SED program across the street and they would come and take him back for two weeks of retooling. Well, he bolted from my room and headed to the principal's office like Quasimodo running into the church for sanctuary. I went into the office where the student was pleading his fantasy case like a combination of Clarence Darrow and Johnny Cochran. The principal dismissed me saying, "I'll handle this." I promptly went over and got the security guard and went back to the principal's office to have Johnny taken across the street. The principal had had a bad day and went ballistic at my overreaching. He had the guard and student wait outside while he chewed me out. I replied with, "Do you wish for me to run my class or would you like to do it yourself? I would be more than happy to have you come down and deal with my students every time there is a problem, which, on average, is every seven minutes." We blinked at each other for a few seconds and then he ordered the security guard to take the young man across the street.

It had dawned upon him that empowering teachers empowers administrators. TEACHERS IN CONTROL OF TEACHING. Whew. I get dizzy just thinking about it. What an astoundingly normal thought that you will be punished for. Thinking such thoughts puts you way out there on the lunatic fringe. Just like the seemingly normal thought of one-man, one-vote. They murdered and fought wars over that one. How dare the poor think that they are equal to the rich? It turned the world and the entire history of the human race upside down. How dare teachers think they can run a classroom? Statements like that will get you into more trouble than John Adams ever dreamed of. I became vice president of the teachers union when I was young, BEFORE I had tenure. Big mistake. Tenure means that once you've taught long enough you are no longer considered a beginning teacher and are now protected by law. The school system has to produce a valid reason for firing you instead of just dumping you in a ditch, like in the good old pre-tenure days. What tenure really means is you can run your mouth if you wish. At least I didn't come home to find my hunting dogs poisoned like the president of the union in a neighboring county did. This whole thing of a teacher being in control of their classroom is such a ridiculous notion. It's as stupid as thinking that a doctor should be in charge of his clinic.

More than just ridiculous, it is genuinely frightening to those non-teachers in charge. To keep teacher's minds off of such things administrators dabble in illusion. Reality is way too hard to deal with, but illusion they've got down. Take the phrase "faculty meeting." You would think that it had something to do with the faculty. They should just call it the principal's meeting and be done with it. I love the phrase "school - based management." It implies that teachers get to have a say about something. The word teacher doesn't appear in the phrase, however, so you're not quite sure. One day in a meeting held on our PLANNING DAY-"planning day" is another good one-I decided to test the waters. I discovered that school-based management means, in plain English, "We are going to write you up and put it in your file." Your permanent file. Your F.B.I. type personnel file, for those of you who take democracy too seriously. It's O.K., though. I like to write, so I wrote back, stapling my letter to their letter. It's sort of like having your own poison pen pal. Well, it's a relationship, anyway. When you're single you take what you can get.

  It wasn't that what I said was out of line, it's that I didn't follow the agenda. You've got the Magna Carta, the Constitution, and the Agenda. It's that sacred. I taught exceptional education for seventeen straight years and the agenda was always the exact same. "We are here to go over the new forms, which are so confusing that we've had to call this meeting on your PLANNING DAY, so that you get this right." You see, if you are an administrator your whole world revolves around paperwork. They view paper as product, as proof that they have done something. The teacher's world, on the other hand, revolves around real, live children. Face time with children is viewed as product, paperwork as anti-product. Don't ever point this inconsistency out unless you want a really thick personnel file.

The first reprimand came when, faced with a pile of new forms, I asked what was wrong with the old forms? I hadn't strayed from the agenda, so I figured I was on safe ground here. Basically, the old forms are old and the new forms are new and everybody knows that new is better than old. I replied that they should run that by their grandmother and monitor the response. Humor is not usually the strong suit of paper pushers, especially when it is coming at the expense of their paper. I didn't make any more remarks about the paper, which set me up for straying from the agenda. I suggested that something be done about students that repeatedly misbehave and disrupt class. They didn't have a plan for that, but I found that they do have one for disruptive adults. They can't do a thing about Tommy cursing, terrorizing the campus, showing his underwear and grabbing Suzie's butt, but they have two dozen legally binding ways to make sure that you keep your mouth shut during a faculty meeting. I eventually ended up going to these meetings dressed accordingly-with a gun taped to my head. This way, when the boredom got unbearable, I had an option. Eventually, I got disinvited to the meetings. I was the only teacher in the county who actually had a planning day.

All of this brings us to a very important point to remember. Teachers are in the exact same relationship to those above as students are to us. Except students have some rights. We're treated like kids who just happened to have found a college degree and a teacher's certificate in the bushes someplace. Don't ever take the phrase "teaching profession" too seriously. It's like the vice-president getting the big head because he's got the word president in his title. Let's compare with a real profession. A fight breaks out in a dentist's office. The dentist calls the police. The thugs are removed. A fight breaks out in the classroom. You call the office. They won't do anything until they see the paperwork. Then you get called down to the office to tell your side of the story because it doesn't match up with the fairy tale that the thug made up. "That's not the way that Jeremy said it happened", as they eyeball you suspiciously, trying to determine who is the liar-Jeremy the little kid or the teacher, the big kid.

 You're even treated like a child when you go away to training conferences. It's not just a local thing. If it's elementary - ed training they talk to you as if you're in the fourth grade. If you're lucky. It's weird. You begin to wonder if you are ever going to get out of school when you realize: no, you're not. Your students will graduate eventually but you are stuck there in some kind of time warp, always being told what to do, always answering to the adults above you. It's strange being treated like a kid when you're fifty. I sat through a training session once where all the teachers had to do a role-playing game. We all wore funny paper hats that had labels on them like "smelly" or "stupid" and you had to guess what your label was by how those around you reacted to your label. Mine evidently read "madder than hell."

 The purpose of these training sessions is to get

points towards the renewal of your teacher certificate. Oh, yes, that certificate you strive so hard for is like Cinderella's coach after five years except that at least you can eat a pumpkin. Unless you get enough points, one hundred and twenty of them, cobbled together by sitting through dozens of meetings being trained by somebody half your age, staying awake by taking bets on who falls asleep first, you lose your certificate. This is the reason for the four industrial - sized coffee pots and the large mountain of sugared products sitting off to the left of every training session. One hundred and twenty points gives you the privilege of staying in the stress factory to polish up your heart problems a little more. Sounds fair to me. It sure makes time fly, though. I don't know about anybody else, but it seems like this anxiety festival comes around monthly.

    I know, deep in my heart, that Rodney Dangerfield had to have been a teacher at some point in his life. A school system is an absolute gold mine for "respect" jokes. Every once in a while something happens that makes me shake my head and wonder if maybe teachers aren't their own worst enemy in this respect thing. Some of the best lessons in life are learned the hard way. This one was pure granite. Back in the middle seventies teacher's were paid $7,800 a year. During this particular year we were offered a $200 a YEAR pay raise. Take it or leave it. The president of the union and myself, the vice-president, called a meeting of all the teachers in the county and gave Patrick Henry-esque speeches. This was the perfect time for arbitration. We had nothing to lose except $4 per week and everything to gain, etc. etc. Let freedom ring. End the injustice. Afterwards we took a secret ballot and it was a landslide. The teachers had voted to take their $4. That's when I struck the word president from my title, kept the word vice and lit out to the nearest bar to figure out what had just happened.

Even so, we don't deserve ALL this disrespect we get. "What's your problem, you get to play with kids all day?" Well, let's see now. The kid just got out of jail. Just exactly what kind of games do you think he wants to play? Another is, "you only have to work ten months out of the year." Everything is relative. How long does ten months defending Omaha Beach feel like to you? "Well, if you can't do, teach." That one is a laugh riot, at least in the mind of the guy hee-hawing about it not two inches from your face. Going postal. Are you kidding me? I am absolutely amazed that it's not "going teacher." Too many letters don't compare with too many students. Ever see the look in a teacher's eye around May tenth? You better do what they say. At a garage sale, if they ask for a dollar off, you better give it to them. Don't argue, just give it to them. You never know what will set them off.

A rotten attitude towards your job can be a life saver. I realize this is not what they teach in college, but it's true. "Sit down, young man, and leave Katrina alone." "Bump you, man. She's my "B"." "I said, sit down, please, or I will personally have to sit you down." "You can't make me. I'll call a lawyer and get you fired." That's when you grab his hand and start kissing it. "Oh, bless you young man. Here's the phone." You start doing some kind of dance number and sing, "free at last, going to make me some money" over and over as you hand it to him. The kid will sit down immediately, guaranteed. "Oh, PLEASE get me fired" works everytime.

I don't understand society anymore. I was at a ball game recently, watching one of my favorite pitchers do his thing. A friend of mine who obviously has way too much time on his hands had recently spent an afternoon figuring out that the pitcher's salary came to $3,000 per pitch. This little bit of information somewhat colored my view of the game. During the third inning alone, he had equaled my entire year's salary. And he WALKED the man. Does anybody have any idea how valuable teachers are to a democratic system? That we are the glue that holds this whole thing together? Now, they won't pay you, but they are well aware of how valuable you are. You can go to jail for even saying the word strike, which is why you have to be very careful at a ball game. Now, a ballplayer can not only say the word strike, but actually do it. "Oh, Mr. Ballplayer, there are some teachers, police officers and nurses here to see you. They would like your autograph. And bring the owner with you. Yes, they're right over there. They're the ones with the torches and pitchforks."

So what is the way out of the woods? I'm not sure. I'm still trying to figure out how and when we let our entire profession get hijacked by people who don't have a single clue as to what teaching is all about. You've got bureaucrats, legislators, governors, congresspeople, and presidents in charge of the whole thing all of whom, after a week at a normal high school, would be found lying in a fetal position, sucking their thumb in a darkened closet. The more they do, the worse it gets, and the worse it gets the more they feel compelled to do. We are stuck in a very bad episode of the Twilight Zone.

Legislators, if you really want to help in the classroom, help in the home. Create a society where parents who are working hard for a living aren't classified as "the working poor." Where a family can afford to actually have one adult member stay at home to raise their children properly-to make sure that they are well fed so that their brains function correctly; so that they aren't raised by violent and disrespectful television; so that they learn proper self-respect and respect for legitimate authority; so they can grow up where violence is not a problem- solving tool; so they can learn that decent, hard work is the way to get ahead in life; so that the American dream is available for all who strive for it. THIS would help the classroom teacher immensely.

To all of you who work in the school system or are thinking about it, God and your students love you. And we've got each other. And with company like that, I can sleep well at night. May God bless all of you, and good night.

BOOK TWO

Addressing Students

School systems would occasionally call Professor Johnson to come speak to troubled students. He would never turn them down, insisting to his college professor colleagues that it was "real teaching", unlike what transpired on campus. He would chide them that it was infinitely easier to teach kids who had actually paid money for it than those with one foot in the failure bucket.

Professor Johnson once explained that to change a kid's behavior you don't tiptoe around issues in which they are already engaged. If they are going to act grown, then talk to them like they're grown. In order for them to actually listen to you they need to trust three things: your motivation for speaking, your knowledge of what you are talking about, and the honesty with which it is delivered. And it better be funny.

Once Professor Johnson was asked if he was ever disappointed at the amount of students who didn't seem to take his lectures to heart. He responded that he was always pleased and amazed at how many that actually did. On the following pages he takes head - on issues that greatly impact society: violence, teen pregnancy, and successful parenting skills. In the words of one of his ex-students, "Professor Johnson delivers." We can't print what he really said, but it was complimentary.

PROFESSOR JOHNSON'S SCREED AGAINST VIOLENCE

Or

How and why a shrimp in diapers can whip your old man.

Preface

Professor Johnson's lecture on the power of nonviolence was given at an In - House Suspension Room at Northville High School in the fall of 2005.

My name is Professor Johnson, and I would like to welcome you to our meeting of the "Might Makes Right Club". This is an O.K. meeting room, I suppose, but it's not nearly as fancy as the main headquarters. That one has bars in the windows. It seems to be an attention grabber, which evidently is needed, because the club members didn't pay any attention to the meetings held on campuses like this one.

Let me look at my index cards here for a couple of seconds. Is there a John Carter here?....... Mr. Carter, I am going to make you club president. It says here that you decided to up the ante and use a weapon in your fight. Sort of "even more might, makes more right." You exemplify the club spirit perfectly and now have a job title. What did you use, anyway? ....A brick? Was it your own, personal brick?........ Oh, you found it. Lucky you. Assault with a deadly weapon sounds much more important than simple battery. When you're in prison, don't tell them it was a brick, though. You'll get laughed at, lose your temper, and without your brick, what are you going to do?

May I see Latresha Shaw? Sweetheart, you are the treasurer. It seems that you are the only one in here with enough sense to fight for personal gain. As smart as you are, this was the best way that you could think of to get money? .... That makes sense. It is the quickest. They don't sell much at the prison shopping mall, however. Then there's always "easy come, easy go." That fits in there somehow.

Who is Michael Brown?....... I see. It is written down here that your excuse is that, and I quote, "you have a temper." Is that correct?......... Could I see it please? .... If I was a surgeon and could cut this temper out of you so that you could live a meaningful and constructive life, where would I begin cutting? ....It's there, but you don't know where. The main thing is you can't control it? Is that what I'm hearing?........... The judge is going to love that. "Yes, you're honor, I have no control over myself. I am, in fact, a ticking time bomb, a menace to society, and I don't mean the movie. Can I go home now?" It all depends on the definition of the word "now". If that means thirty years, then yes. I have a temper. I love that. You better buy a leash for it. You are now the sergeant at arms. This will give you the opportunity to work with other behavioral challenged individuals who have lost their temper. Perhaps you can help them find it. It probably rolled up under their seat there, someplace.

I am happy to be here this morning, and I will tell you why. I can look into your eyes and tell that I am not dealing with crazy people. I am dealing with young men and women who are destined for greatness later on in life. I know it. I can feel it. I would not be here wasting my time if I felt otherwise. I am not dealing with crazy people OR stupid people. I AM dealing with people who have a near empty toolbox with which to solve their problems. At the end of the next two hours I hope to leave you with a toolbox that is fuller and more effective. One that you can carry with you for the rest of your life.

Let's open the toolbox that you carry with you now. Well, lookee here, it's not empty, like some of your teachers might say, but it has only one tool in it. Let's see what it is. It is, of course, the hammer. "Honey, would you fix the TV set, please?" No problem. Crash, crash, crash. "All fixed, dear." "The baby is crying. Could you put her to sleep, please." No problem. Crash, crash, crash. "She's asleep, dear." The hammer is great for some things, but not EVERYTHING. And if the only emotional tool that you have in your toolbox is anger and violence then you will not solve ANY of your problems.

The first lesson of today is VIOLENCE IS NOT A PROBLEM SOLVING TOOL. Let's examine that. Pick something to fight about. Yes? .... That's a good one. Girls. Frederick and Jeremy are madly in love with the same girl. We'll call her Bathsheba. What to do about this age old problem? How about beat each other to a bloody pulp? That's the ticket to her heart. So, Frederick and Jeremy call each other out and go at it right in the middle of the school, thus providing entertainment for the entire student body. These are not selfish young men. I'm rooting for Jeremy here, because Frederick is kind of a jerk and probably wouldn't treat Bathsheba right, anyway. What is the very BEST outcome for Jeremy? That he wins the fight, right? He is the man. He has sent Frederick to the hospital and thrashed a couple of his cousins too, so that Frederick won't get lonesome in the critical ward. Jeremy has now won the girl and would like to take her out but can't because the police are stuffing him into the police car. He does end up with a nice girlfriend in prison, though, but his name is Frank.

That didn't exactly turn out as expected, so let's

try the other scenario. What is the very WORST outcome for Jeremy? Jeremy wakes up in the hospital and looks like a plastic surgeon worked on him in reverse. He is now so ugly that he couldn't get a date anymore, with Bathsheba OR Frank.

At least both young men are still alive. What sometimes happens is the big, tearful, "I didn't mean it" scenario. Somebody is in the cemetery and the other has "I didn't mean it" tattooed on the inside of his brain until he finally joins his ex-friend.

Did any of this solve Jeremy's problem? Of course not. While these two morons are fighting, Bathsheba ran off with Kelvin, who has his own car and has a steady stream of money, because he is employed.

Violence will NEVER solve your problem, but is almost always guaranteed to compound it. Taking the violence road is the one way to insure that you'll never reach your destination. The strange part is that the people who insist upon taking that road are always shocked when they end up on some weird detour. "Wait a minute, this isn't Bathsheba's house. This looks like a courtroom. How did I get here?"

Let me digress for a minute. I was teaching my Sunday school class one day and I asked my students a question: Why be polite? I mean, really. Why expend all this energy going around being polite to people you don't even know or might not even like? It's a lot more fun being rude and a whole lot more entertaining. A whole television empire has been built on it. So, why be polite? This young man looked at me and said, "to get what you want." This blew my mind. The first thing that I thought of was, "why didn't I think of that?" and the second was, "that is the most perfect definition of power I've ever heard of": THE ABILITY TO GET WHAT ONE WANTS.

Taking that definition, let's examine how to get REAL power, which is control over your life. Let's start with "please" and "thank you." ....What do you mean "you're kidding?". These are two of the most powerful words in the English language. I can see by your laughter that you don't believe me. It's true ....So, you think that being polite is begging. And begging, of course, is beneath your dignity. You know, a lot of kids think like that. You're not alone on this one. I had a young man once who demanded that I turn on the air conditioner in class. "Mr. Johnson, turn on the air conditioner, it's hot in here!" I raised an eyebrow at his tone and agreed with him that it was indeed hot in the classroom. I went on teaching. "Didn't you hear me? I said it's hot in here!" "Yes, it is, as evidenced by the fact that I am sweating like a pig up here. Now, if you will ask me properly, I would be more than happy to turn on the air conditioner." I had my own dignity to think about. I continued teaching. One young man, thinking that he was being helpful, leaned forward and told him, "He wants you to say, please." "I know what he wants. I ain't begging for nobody. Begging days are gone." "What's up with that? Just tell the man "please." "Please?" "No way." Now the entire class started to get surly, because they realized that this guy would rather have everybody roast to death than do the right thing. I think it was "tell the man "please" or else I'll wring your neck like a chicken" that finally turned the tide.

What on earth was that all about? I find myself asking that a lot these days, which is not a good sign for society. I also answer my own questions, living alone and all, which is probably not a good sign for my own mental health. But this is what I think. I think that a lot of students these days are overly anxious to be grown up, just like all the generations before them. And they resent being treated like a kid, who has about as much say over his life as I have over the orbit of the moon. From this point of view, politeness equals being weak, because it is just for kids, and rudeness and intimidation are seen as strength, because you are FORCING people to do your bidding. This makes a child feel powerful, or grown up. The problem is, while on this journey for respect, the student is holding the road map upside down and ends up wondering how he got lost in the woods someplace, because this rudeness thing NEVER WORKS and you end up spending every minute of the day butting heads with somebody because you are constantly making even the simplest things a battle of wills.

Let's start with respect, which is what all of this is about, anyway. You will never get respect by demanding it. You can produce fear, which a lot of people mistake for respect, but you will never get respect. You have to give respect to get respect. Try this when you get home tonight. "Mom, where's the food?" Scream "I'M HUNGRY. I WANT TO EAT NOW" at the top of your lungs and see if you get to eat immediately, not at all, or wear your meal on your head.

At your first job interview, give this a shot: GIVE ME THE JOB BECAUSE I'LL TURN YOUR CAR INTO A ROASTING MARSHMALLOW IF YOU DON'T. Let me know how your job goes - I mean the one folding the laundry at the county jail.

Young lady, could I please borrow your pencil for a second?....... Thank you. See how easy that was? And I now, in fact, have a pencil in my hand. I have turned my wishes into reality. I am a powerful person. Politeness is not for children. You teach it to children so that they know how to act as adults. Politeness is a social respect contract for all adults everywhere. It confers automatic respect between adults, including complete strangers. Instant respect. Give it, get it. If I say, "Thank you very much" after being handed food in the cafeteria I have just respected that woman for all the hard work she had done that day. If I say, "This food looks like diarrhea" I am now wearing a food hat again.

Since power is the ability to get what you want, the search for real power starts with respect. Self-respect and the respect for others. Everything is built on the foundation of respect. Which means, if we think about it, that power is an INTERNAL thing, something you carry inside of you. Those without any real power use an external power source such as a knife or gun, to make up for the lack of it. More on that later. Power is how you carry yourself. How you carry yourself directly effects how people react to you. You, in effect, set up your own reality around you by how you carry yourself. Let me glance at these cards again for a minute. It seems that a couple of you have developed quite a list of enemies in a very short time span. We've got two fights, three fights, two fights. Here's a good one, five fights. Mr. Rowley, I assume you are getting paid for this? .... Well, we need to have a talk with your guidance counselor, because fighting for free is a lousy career choice......I see. It's that everybody hates you. I hear you. I remember my high school days well. I still occasionally wake up screaming in the middle of the night.

Let's talk about the law of Kharma. Anybody ever hear of that? I believe it's Hindu, and I believe that it is as real as the laws of gravity or inertia. Kharma?......... Very good. "What goes around, comes around." No truer words were ever spoken. How do they say the same thing in the Christian religion? There are several sayings to chose from. ...."Live by the sword, die by the sword." Excellent. What else?............. "Do unto others." My personal favorite is "you reap what you sow." I believe that if you study any major religion, they all have a version of this law of REALITY. Let's do a little visual aid thing here. I'm going to write on the board three configurations. One is plus/plus, one is plus/minus and the last is minus/minus. There we go . The plus meaning happy, positive people, the minus meaning unhappy, negative people. Charles, come up here please. Let's see what happens when two pluses meet. "Charles, how was the ball game last night?.......... What do you mean, you didn't see it? This is pretend here..............That's great. I loved it too, especially the goal line stand.

Great seeing you again. Take care, now."

Now let's try out the plus/minus. I'll let Charles be the minus on this one, which is usually a lot more fun, at least until you get punched in the face. We're walking down the hall and we accidently bump into each other. O.K., let's go. .... "Hey, watch where you're going you fool! You want a piece of me?" "I'm sorry, my bad. I was busy staring at Barbara walking to class." I go on, nothing happens. Now comes the real fun. We both get to be negative. Let's walk down the hall again. "Who are you bumping into, you fool?" "Fool is it? If you weren't such an epileptic, you could probably walk properly." "Why don't you shut up?" "Why don't you make me?" Now, this leads to the most famous Hindu saying of them all: "It takes two to Tango." Is there going to be a fight in this hallway today? Of course there is. Two thunder clouds have just met and there will be lightening. I am sure that neither Mr. Negative came to school to fight that day. "You reap what you sow." If you spend all day putting out negative, don't be startled when your harvest bears a bitter fruit as the philosopher The Shadow would say.

Those of you who are in constant conflict with others may want to do a little self-examination and look at what kind of kharma grid that you are putting out. Many young people these days watch a LOT of television and advertising. I worry about all those images showing men being hard, not smiling, the new ferocious man, like that is supposed to be attractive. If you walk around looking like that all day long, it's a wonder that you make it back from school alive each day. Just say to yourself, it's only TV, it's only TV. I mean, really. If you're in the grocery store and one cashier is smiling and waving at you to come through her line and the other one is snarling at an old lady because she isn't counting her change fast enough, which one are you going to go to?

There are three sources of power available to everyone. I'll write these down. You've got physical power, intellectual power, and character/spiritual power. Let's look at everybody's favorite number one go-to source, physical power. This is the brand "A" power source for five year olds, because they haven't had the time yet to cultivate the others. If you are fifteen and this is still your brand "A" power source you are in deep trouble because brand "A" is no power source at all. It is the ILLUSION of power, but is in fact a very seductive trap. You will end up powerless, whether in jail, in the hospital, in the cemetery, or if you're lucky, just sitting in a room on Saturday being bored out of your skull, while your friends are at the mall right now flirting with your boy and girlfriends.

Physical strength. I'll say one thing for it, it sure looks good. It sure feels good. Let's go back in time - It's 1846. You are a slave. Are you strong? .... I know you're white, use your imagination. Are you strong?......... Of course you are. That is what the man paid the big money for. Were there laws against weight lifting, against getting stronger? Of course not. Were you, in fact, powerful? ....You were, were you? Are you kidding me? You are a SLAVE. Does somebody of color want to pick this one up? Would a dictionary help here? One of the definitions is, and I quote, "one who has lost all powers of resistance." I'll shorten that up for those of you with short sound - bite attention spans. "One who has lost all power." Go to any prison in America, and what are half of these guys doing all day long? Pumping iron. Working on their power source, like anybody cares. They are IN A CAGE, powerless to effect any kind of change in the real world. There were no laws against weight lifting in 1846, but I'll tell what laws they did have, to cut off the REAL power source. It was AGAINST THE LAW to teach slaves how to read. And this was not a misdemeanor, fifty dollar fine type of law. It was the hang you in the middle of the town square so that everybody in the county can see we mean it, type of law. Now we are talking about INTELLECTUAL power. If you go to a prison, the only one that strikes any fear into anybody's heart is the guy who spends all his time in the library. THAT is the guy to watch out for. The entire idea of a police officer having to read you your rights, the Miranda ruling, was hatched out of the head of an angry prisoner who could also read well. Look at our entire economic system. Hercules could carry boulders from point "A" to point "B" for an entire hour and have four dollars to show for it, after taxes.

    Physical strength, by and of itself, is just about worthless as a power source. It does make you look cool in a bathing suit, however. The only time that it seems like a good idea to go there is in an attempt to get your way through violence or intimidation, which is mental violence. Once you go there, however, you have completely shut down your two real power sources, intellect and character.

I don't know how to break this to you, but fighting isn't what it used to be. Unfortunately, every teenager in the world has a brain defect that clouds the judgement. It is the unyielding belief that you are invincible. Every last child that I have counseled for fighting has taken offense to the notion that they might actually have something happen to them that isn't quite TV-like. They don't take offense to the suggestion that fighting is wrong, or that hurting other people is wrong or that embarrassing their entire family is wrong, but they will get downright angry if it is suggested that they are a mortal human being; are, in fact, a member of the human race. That doesn't sit well with them, at all. They are willing to fight all over again, just to prove their point, which is that they are living in La-La land and are perfectly happy there and are unhappy living here on Earth.

Mr. Randolph, would you please come up here and give us a demonstration of what a human fighting machine can do. Now, keep in mind that I am a defenseless old man, so everything we do will be in slow motion. And pretend. That pretend part is important. O.K., you stand over there and we will get into a fight over something significant, like a girl said that you said that her boyfriend said bad things about her. Here we go. What is the first thing you do? .... Oh, come on now. Everybody knows it's take off your shirt. What are you laughing for? You know I'm right. I would like for somebody to explain to me why they do that. I mean, you are putting yourself in the position of getting beat to a pulp and looking like

Ygor for the rest of your life and you are worried about if you are going to have a clean shirt to wear to the hospital? ....That's alright, you don't have to explain it. It makes perfect sense to me. Right up there with this invincible thing. Let's go, off with the shirt, in slow motion. Now, when his shirt reaches right about here, is when I pull my gun out and BANG!. Now I start dancing around like Ali, because this fight is over. NEXT!

Your main problem is, you're not insane. You are a normal guy getting caught up in something stupid. Not everyone one is normal. In a fight you've got crazy, crazier and craziest. Which one is going to win? Except you can't use the word "win", because the crazier you are, the more jail time you get. The last time I went to a real bar-Hooters doesn't count- was a long time ago. I saw two guys who both had minus signs all over them discover each other, which they always seem to do, using their hate radar I presume, and they started to go at it. I left around the time that the less crazy of the two was getting his nose bit off.

I love all of you in this room. I don't ever want to open up my newspaper and read anything about you but your graduation notice. You need to respect yourself and don't put yourself in dangerous positions. It is not a sign of cowardice, it is a sign of intelligence, which is the power source that you need to go to every once in a while. Even superman has to watch out for kryptonite.

A word on weapons here. There are a LOT of powerless people these days who want to be the man, and don't really know how to do it. With so many boys being raised in fatherless families, it's kind of hard to figure out how to do it. For only a few dollars you can buy at least a pretend manhood, just stick a gun in your pocket. The power surge you get is enormous. I can stick a gun in a baby's diaper and he will start crawling around like John Wayne. If you look closely, however, he still drools and cries at the drop of a hat, and is no closer to manhood than before he added the two pounds of metal. It is the illusion of power that makes a gun especially dangerous, because the reality is the exact opposite. I was listening to National Public Radio once and heard an interview with an ex-gang leader from New York City, and he explained why he was on a one man mission to get rid of guns. When he carried one, he found himself heading into crazy, dangerous situations instead of doing what normal people do, which is run for their life. The gun made him a trouble magnet. It also has the opposite effect of protecting yourself. It, in fact, makes you a human bull's - eye. You end up finding yourself in places you shouldn't be, yelling at people that you shouldn't be yelling at and then wondering why every night is a replay of the O.K. Corral. Do you know why nobody on the planet hates the Swiss? It's because they don't have a giant arsenal that threatens the existence of life on the planet earth. If they come unhinged, what's the worst that could happen? They close their ski-resorts?

  A gun in your pocket screams to be used, just like money. Ever see a little kid with ten dollars that wasn't begging to spend it? On ANYTHING?

"Please, dad, let me buy that necktie. It's a nice one." "NO. Save your money for something you really want." "O. K. How about this blender?" You are going to find yourself making up any excuse in this world to shoot the gun, or at least wave it around, because what good is your only claim on manhood if nobody knows that you have got it?

I suppose that makes a girl's claim to womanhood the razor. If a girl starts reaching for her shoe in the middle of a fight, it is probably not to tie up the dangling shoelace. Getting into an argument with another girl over somebody's boyfriend, who is probably cheating on the both of them in the first place, and walking away looking like a jack-o-lantern for the rest of your life is not going to land the guy of your dreams, unless he's Freddie Kruger.

VIOLENCE IS THE ENEMY. Violence itself. Not you. Not the person you're having a dispute with. Violence as a problem solving tool. Don't EVER make the mistake of thinking that you are its master. That you can control it. History is littered with fools that think that they could control violence. How about a little slap-fest called, and I'm not making this up, the HUNDRED YEARS WAR. I wonder if they planned it that way? All this foolishness bankrupted the French, which led to the French Revolution, which is the poster child for violence run amuck. Off with their heads. Which heads? Well, after awhile, ANY head will do. The beast must be fed.

Hatfields and the McCoys. Well, let's put our families in the history books by shooting at each other FOR GENERATIONS because of a dispute OVER A

PIG. Brilliant move.

The fact that violence is it's own living, breathing entity which springs to life through the minds of people that have few problem solving skills is actually incased in law. In 1926 Clarence Darrow, probably the greatest defense attorney that ever lived, defended a black man named Dr. Sweet who had moved into an all white neighborhood in Detroit. A white mob formed outside the house for several days. One of the members of the Sweet family fired shots through the window at the mob killing one man and wounding another. Eleven black people in the house were arrested for first degree murder. Clarence Darrow won the case, even though no shots were fired first from the white mob, because a mob HAS A LIFE OF IT'S OWN. VIOLENCE has a life of its own. It is the fear of that underlying threat of violence that allowed Dr. Sweet to be acquitted. I remember when I was in junior high school. I was talking with a guy that was a friend of mine and, for whatever reason, we started arguing about something. Other kids started gathering around and before I knew it, the crowd was taking sides and pumping up a fight. To my shame, I pushed the young man and he pushed me back. You could feel the hate engine being revved up. We looked at each other, fists balled up. I then looked at the mob around me and then back at my friend. I got mad at being put in this situation, where there was no real graceful way out. Fortunately, I was madder at the jerks around me than at my friend and I pushed myself through the crowd and went to class. I was fully prepared to spend the rest of my day in abject humiliation, but it didn't turn out that way. The crowd pretty much gave a collective, "Oh, well, no entertainment today" and went on about their way. My friend was just as relieved as I was that nothing stupid had happened and we laughed at what boneheads we were later on. I will never forget what the rising of the violence beast felt like, however. I was just very lucky that it didn't get fed that day.

Since violence itself is the enemy, what are we going to do about it? The human race, which seems hardwired for all kinds of vicious insanity, has been grappling with this one for eons. I am fixing to load your toolbox with some other tools to reach for besides the hammer. First, a little more history. There are a few great people down through the ages who became great by tackling this issue head on. A theory of nonviolence as a powerful problem solving tool has been developed, used and perfected by Martin Luther King Jr. to change the entire course of United States history for the better. Understanding what he did and how he did it will change your life, because it goes to the real meaning and source of power. To get to Martin Luther King Jr., however, we have to go through three other gentlemen first.............So you think this is boring? Are you kidding me? We get to talk about people getting tacked up to trees, being thrown in jail, beaten and shot. You'd sleep through an earthquake, wouldn't you? I will make it brief, however, because I realize that the mall is calling your name.

We are going to discuss four weak, sissy crybabies who also happen to be the most powerful men on earth. What separates them from everybody else is that they discovered the seemingly bizarre notion that love is more powerful than hate. Not nicer, MORE POWERFUL. They harnessed this love force to change the world. Now, since everybody's vision of manhood is wrapped up in being harder than an industrial diamond, this is all going to seem very weird. AT FIRST. Hang with me here. I'm going to show you what manhood is all about, never mind the fact that half of these guys seem to be dressed in diapers, and one's a hippie lunatic.

You can start your eyes rolling here, because I am going to give you a quick, HISTORICAL perspective of Jesus Christ. This is not church here and there are dozens of way cool religions that profess many of the same values, but to understand people like REVEREND Martin Luther King Jr., you need to understand what Jesus Christ brings to the table, because in many ways it was a turning point for a slice of mankind.

The Old Testament, of which I'm sure you're all intimately familiar, is filled with violence, depravity and revenge. That's because Christ is nowhere to be found in it. The bible double clutches and throws itself into reverse in the New Testament, with the introduction of Jesus, who is the living embodiment of the love force. When asked what was the single most important thing that God expects of humans, he responded with "love thy neighbor." Asked to distill it even further, since evidently this was a little murky, he implied that God is LOVE. Period. This came as an awful shock to the system, since this seemed to go against the grain of what humans are all about, which is violence, depravity and revenge. They knew that he was insane when he was asked what to do about violence, and he responded with "turn the other cheek." So they did what any self respecting human would do when faced with insanity, they tacked his cheek and everything else to a tree.

Fast forward to 1846. Now you've got the grandfather of all hippies, Henry David Thoreau, who is thinking all kinds of crazy thoughts. This happens when you live all by yourself in the woods in a house of your own making, for years. WAY too much time to think. They didn't have all these electronic gadgets back then to steadily bombard the brain with SOMETHING, ANYTHING, to wash away the deadly silence, which is the birthplace of thought. So this guy's brain is in overdrive and he actually thinks that war and violence are WRONG, and he is not going to support a government that thinks that war and violence are good foreign policy, so he totally loses his mind, and refuses to pay his taxes. Fortunately for him, humans had evolved beyond the tree-tacking stage into the much more humane put-'em-in-a-cage-until-they-rot stage.

Besides being a crusty old hermit, he was a brilliant writer. I am going to quote briefly from his treatise "On the DUTY of Civil Disobedience", which is the virtual constitution of the power through non-violence movement. "A common and natural result of an undue respect for law is, that you may see a file of soldiers, colonel, captain, corporal, privates, powder-monkeys and all, marching in admirable order over hill and dale to the wars, against their wills, aye, against their common sense and consciences, which makes it very steep marching indeed, and produces a palpitation of the heart. They have no doubt that it is a damnable business in which they are concerned; they are all peaceably inclined. Now what are they? Men at all?" * ....I'll continue farther on. "The mass of men serve the state thus, not as men mainly, but as machines, with their bodies......In most cases there is no exercise whatever of the judgement or of the moral sense; but they put themselves on a level with earth and wood and stones; and wooden men can perhaps be manufactured that will serve the purpose as well. Such command no more respect than men of straw or a lump of dirt." * Holy mackerel! No wonder they put this guy in jail. He was a truly dangerous man. I bet you never heard nothing like that on television. Corporations are not overly eager to have their logos identified with dangerous ideas. Bad for business. If you don't do anything else, you students need to learn how to read and read well.

    The man is dangerous because he is powerful. His ideas have the ability to effect real change in the world. His power comes from his intellectual ability, his ability to coherently express his thoughts, and then doubles by combining with the third power source, that of character.

    What was he saying? One thing he did was redefine manhood. His definition does not include

---

* Footnote - Henry David Thoreau, <u>Civil Disobedience</u>, published by The American Liberty, New York, 1960: 20th Printing, pgs. 223-224.
* Ibid

physical strength, but the strength of DOING THE RIGHT THING, NO MATTER WHAT ANYBODY ELSE THINKS, AND NO MATTER WHAT THE COST. The next thing he did was define violence as unnatural, unmanly and wrong. The sounds you hear are the far-away echoes of Jesus Christ. And what got him stuffed in a jail was the gall to suggest that you weren't any kind of a man who could look himself in the mirror in the morning without retching at the coward that was staring back at you unless you did what you could to STOP the violence. Which, in a perverse kind of way meant that if you were involved in violence and you knew that it is wrong YOU WERE THE COWARD. Violence is an act of cowardice. Walking away is not. Now we are going to have a moment of silence here while we let that little brainblow sink in.

And the thing is, I know it's true and so do you. It was much easier for me to push my friend than to say in front of everybody that what was happening was wrong. MUCH easier, which is why I did it. I was in fact a COWARD at the time, because I would rather hurt somebody than face the scorn of my peers. I have seen kids lie, cheat, steal, assault and murder because they were afraid not to. Afraid of what somebody might say. Afraid to stand up to the bully, because then he may turn his bully butt on you. I hear you. Welcome to the human race.

Fast forward a hundred years or so, and we meet a gentleman who was confronted with a problem. He was living in India, a country that had been taken over by the British Empire, the most powerful empire the planet had ever seen. Just ask them, they'll tell you. His name was Mahatma Ghandi. He looked like he had a birth weight of nine ounces and dressed like it for the rest of his life. How you attract women older than two wearing a diaper, I don't know, but he had more pressing things on his mind, like bringing an empire to it's knees, by himself. Force wasn't an option. The Empire wrote the book on the use of force. How about read a book and get some wild ideas into your head? He studied Thoreau and realized that this nonviolent civil disobedience thing might just work if you could find a few million people crazy enough to go along with you. This is where the character thing comes in, because you can't even get more than two people to agree on what to eat for lunch unless they have faith in YOU. People of intellect and character have figured out what drives people with intellect and no character: MONEY. If money is somebody's sole motivation for getting up in the morning, then you've got them right where you want them. Choke off that money supply, nonviolently, and it is amazing how all of a sudden you are now dealing with somebody full of character, willing to do the right thing. Just turn the money faucet back on. Quickly, please. They don't CARE if the money comes from right or wrong, so force them to do it the right way, and make it impossible to do it the wrong way. They're still happy, and you've got your freedom. Ghandi got millions of people to boycott British goods, taught people to make their own clothes, got salt from the sea, WHATEVER, just so you didn't pay the British for anything. If he had taken up arms against the British, India might still be a member of the empire, with its citizens drinking tea at twelve while doing their best to ignore the explosions and the occasional mass murder. The moral of this story is that NONVIOLENCE works to get your way and violence DOESN'T.

To finish beating this dead horse, I am going to end with Martin Luther King Jr., for whom everybody in this country owes an everlasting debt. He is literally the founding father of modern, relatively conflict-free, America. Before I discuss what happened at Birmingham, however, I am going to give you a little visual aid on the power of nonviolence.

Mr. Randolph, my slow-motion fighting machine, could you please come back up here for a minute?........ No, I'm not going to shoot you in the stomach again. Besides, you've been sitting too long, anyway. O.K., here we go again. But this time, I am going to defend myself with judo. Come back here. I will pretend if you will pretend. Now, does anybody know what judo is? .... No, that's karate, where you actually get to hit somebody. Judo is the art of self-defense ONLY. No hitting. It is also a philosophy in which you use your aggressor's violence against himself, or herself, if your date has gone sour on you. Alright, throw the punch. You notice how I avoid the blow, take his arm like so, and by moving my hip I can throw him clean up against the wall? The beauty of it is that the harder he tries to hit me, the farther I can throw him. I use his own violence as a weapon against him. The crazier he gets, the more he gets hurt. Keep this in mind, because now I am going to talk about Birmingham. Thank you, Mr. Randolph. You can peel yourself off the wall and have a seat now.

The civil rights march on Birmingham was a watershed in American history. You had hundreds of protesters in full Martin Luther King Jr. mode, singing and praying. Not a gun, knife or fingernail clipper in sight. Singing and praying. Martin Luther King Jr. made a huge point of this. He trained people for moments like this, because turning the other cheek absolutely does not come naturally or easily. He knew that if their was any violence on THEIR PART that the entire battle for real democracy in the United States would be lost. What was waiting for these peaceful people was a butt whipping of gigantic proportions and it was not going to be pretty, WHICH WAS THE POINT. On television the entire country was treated to the spectacle of men, women and children being attacked by police dogs, beaten with clubs and the old stand-by, thrown in jail. In that short time frame, however, the worm began to turn. Judo on a mass scale was being performed to a world-wide audience. The violence, which was so near and dear to the racists, was used against them. All over America, while people were watching the nightly news, you had conversations like this: "I don't know Elmer, that don't look quite right to me. I mean, I might be a stone cold racist with a heart the size of a shriveled lima bean but whipping up on somebody's grandmother just don't seem fair. At least turn off the water cannon and let her stand up and try to get a couple of licks in." The violence was so ugly compared to the non-violence that the civil rights movement was able to eventually throw that part of America against the wall, so to speak. And you, personally, may want to keep somewhere in the back of your mind that fighting makes you look like Peter the Pinhead the next time you want to beat up on somebody.

As an aside, sometimes you find yourself shaking your head. The only evidence I see for evolution NOT being true is that chimpanzees and apes don't go on monkeycidle rampages whenever they can't get their way, unlike us highly developed and evidently high-strung humans.

On a personal note, it amazes me that to this very day there are some people who regard Martin Luther King Jr. as being weak. This usually comes from the "violence is a good idea" crowd.. Well, King had a very strong gut feeling that he wasn't going to be coming back from his trip to Memphis, but felt that it was his duty to go ANYWAY. If that is not the definition of manhood, I don't know what is. Gary Cooper got an academy award for it in High Noon.

Since violence is the last refuge of the powerless trying desperately to make themselves heard, how do you go about becoming really, truly, powerful? How can you get your way in life? I am going to use a four letter word here, which I don't normally do, but it is WORK. You have to work at it. Most violent people are simply lazy. They are going to take the shortest route possible to success city, except that they never reach the city gates. And again, this always seems to come as a surprise to them.

If fighting is not going to get you anyplace, what should you WORK at that will? Start with your intellect. Your brain. There is money in them there squiggles. Lots of it. Read, write, explore math. If a class is boring, get over it. Tape a twenty dollar bill to the top of your desk to remind you of why you are being bored. People will pay you wheel barrels full of money to do things that they can't. I have got to pay some joker forty dollars an hour to work on my car, because I don't even know what I'm looking at anymore when I stare helplessly under the hood. I shell out over two hundred dollars an hour to have some lady tell me to calm down, because it's a pimple and not skin cancer. When I'm ready to pitch my computer out into the backyard I pay good money for somebody to talk me out of it. A huge part of the reason why you are in this room today is not because you're stupid, but you have no faith in yourself. You have no self-respect. You don't think that you have the ability to make money using your brain. SURE YOU DO. I have a picture on my wall of a young Hispanic lady. She is standing next to a large, double prop airplane. During World War Two she would fly the plane into combat areas, swoop down and pick up the wounded, fly them back to the hospital, and then change her clothes quickly so that she could operate on them, because she was also a surgeon. ARE YOU KIDDING ME? The woman looks like she's fifteen in the picture. YOU CAN DO ANYTHING YOU WANT TO DO. What is it that you want to do? Almost invariably, whenever I ask that question of children who have gotten themselves into some kind of serious trouble, the answer is "I don't know." What they are really saying is "I don't have any idea whatsoever why some universal power has stuck me on this planet. It must be some kind of a cosmic joke. I am here by accident." No wonder you feel powerless. Find your purpose, find your power. I have a suggestion that might help. SMASH YOUR TV. SMASH YOUR GANGSTER CDs. Stop brainwashing yourself into being a violent, disrespectful idiot. Have faith in yourself that you can actually earn a good living and be helpful to others at the same time. YOU CAN DO IT.

I had a young man as a student who was the best welder we had seen come through the vocational school in a long time. He was on his way to making thirty-five dollars an hour, minimum. Young lady, what is eight times thirty? ....Remember that for me please. Young man, eight times five?...... And if I put those two together, what have I got? .... Two hundred and eighty dollars. That is per day, if the student had the ability to run his own business and weld for himself, and I believe he did. Anybody in here want to walk home with almost three hundred dollars? Everyday?..... I thought so. One evening I got a phone call at my house from this young man, which I thought a little strange, since most students aren't so thrilled with school that they want to drag it out into the night. He apologized, but said that he was going to be absent for a while. I asked how long. When he responded three to five years, I realized that he was calling from the jail. He had shot into an occupied car when his midnight business transaction didn't go exactly as planned. What a waste. His life. My time. All because he didn't have any faith that game plan "A" was going to get him anywhere so he jumped to game plan "Z", what we refer to in the sports business as fumbling the football on the one yard line.

Which leads to your other power source, that of

character. Evidently intellect alone isn't going to cut it. Intellect without character will get you into trouble every time. Not only do you think you're smarter that anybody else, but actually SUPERIOR. You don't have to follow the same rules as everybody else. This is a seriously dangerous illusion, for both you and all the lesser human beings around you. Every single person in jail will tell you the same thing. I didn't think I'd get caught. The Enron boys sobbing how sorry they are? They didn't realize that others would take offense at them ruining the lives of hundreds of thousands of people? Oh, really?

Your character is your highest form of power. Intellect will get you a job. Character allows you to keep it. What is the first and foremost thing that a business person wants from you? It's not to do a good job. It's that you won't rob them blind when they are not paying attention. THEN, it's do a good job. The definition of character is what you do when nobody is looking. What, in fact, you really are at your core. Doing the right thing, all the time, to the best of your ability will get you places that strength and intellect can't even imagine. This idea is at the center of how the universe works.

I worked at a mental retardation center for a year and probably spent the first nine months wishing that they would call it something else. Anyway, I had a young man that we shall call John brought to me from somebody in the community. They wanted me to train him for a job that he was trying to get at a local fast food place. John was seriously challenged. He got "small" and "large" without too much of a struggle, but I thought that the concept of "medium" was going to kill us both. After snatching myself baldheaded, he was ready for work. The other thing about John is that he is, hands down, the nicest human being I have ever met. If a nuclear war had taken out the entire city, you would find John standing in the middle of the rubble with smoldering charcoal briquette hamburgers in each hand, a huge smile on his face, asking what he could do for you that day. He has kept that job for twenty years.

People can train skills, but it is infinitely harder to train character. That is going to have to come from you, and your view of yourself. Are you in this room because you are a bad person or are you here because you are a good person who is all too human and has down something bad? Is your condition permanent or temporary? That is the only question that really matters and the one that everybody in the human race needs to answer for themselves. What do YOU think of you?

Father Flanigan, who founded Boys Town, once said that there was no such thing as a bad child. I agree with him. That is not so important as whether or not you agree with him.

I am looking at a room of powerful people. What are you going to do with your new-found power? How are you going to deal with violence when it rears its ugly head? You need to come up with a PLAN. An anti-violence plan. If you don't have a plan, then you are planning to fight. Guaranteed.

What did Ghandi and King do first? ORGANIZE. There is strength in numbers. Show some leadership. Combine intellect with character. If there is not a real, coherent plan in your school to deal with the specter of bullying and violence, demand one. Start one. Most schools have a violence plan, but it's not very good. It's called "Boy, that was horrifying and I hope it doesn't happen again." There is a concept called peer mediation, where students such as yourselves are trained to mediate conflicts BEFORE they turn ugly. There are teen courts. There are tangible reward systems for the use of nonviolence as a power tool. Start them. Use your student council as a real voice. VOTE. I am going to say that again, because it is the real power source that is available to everybody. VOTE. As a student. As an adult. There is a reason why untold thousands have been murdered globally in their quest for the right to vote. IT IS A REAL SOURCE OF POWER and don't let anyone tell you otherwise. They are not murdering and jailing people for the fun of it. The concept of one-person one-vote is a direct and dangerous challenge to the other concept of power, "money talks and everybody else walks." Actually, it's "crawls", but that doesn't rhyme. There is one place and one place only where the rich and poor are equal and that is in the voting booth.

    My suggestion is, if you don't exercise your right to vote, don't complain about NOTHING. If you are that lazy, then there is the reason why you've got a bunch of stuff to complain about. I learned several lessons while running for county commission, lesson one being whiners don't vote. They whine. At first I would listen to people's complaints for hours on end.

"My road needs fixing. The taxes are too high. There are no jobs." Only afterwards would I find out that the last time they voted was for Dwight D. Eisenhower. Or better yet, they have never even bothered to register. If you guys want to brush up on your lame-o excuses for not doing your homework go out onto the campaign trail. There is a reason why some people live on lousy roads and are jobless. They even lack the creativity to come up with a lousy excuse.

If voting doesn't make you drunk with power then actually have the guts to turn off the TV and run for office. Don't look so shocked. Yes, YOU. Run for office at school, run as an adult. You want power, go for it. Not only is this not crazy, but it is actually doable.

I remember walking the streets with a young man, barely out of school, who had the insane notion of trying to become the first black Clerk of the Courts ever in my county. We would be walking door to door and I kept wondering what was that strange clacking sound I heard? I finally realized that it was his knees knocking. I recognized it because they made the same sound mine did when I went door to door during my quest for a county commission seat. He has been in office for years now with a wall full of plaques and accolades. I taught the sheriff in town when he was in the fourth grade. Even then he said that he wanted to be a police officer. He ran for office to become the first black sheriff in the history of the county. He's well on the way to being the best sheriff in the state.

If running for office isn't your cup of tea, have a dream and go for it. A friend of mine was the only female captain of a firefighting department in the state of Florida. If you dream it, and it is positive, and you are willing to work for it, it is do-able. You can make it real. Real power lies inside of each and everyone of you. Have faith in yourself. Respect yourself. Don't be lazy. And don't fight. I mean, give me a break. Men, if you feel the need to prove your manhood, just take a quick look down your pants. It's there. You don't have to prove it. And fighting leads to undignified scenes. I saw a young man who was trying to fight while holding his pants up. There is a reason why professional boxers use both hands. Being knocked out with your pants around your ankles is not going to win points with your girlfriend, trust me on this one.

    Leave the fighting to HBO. Go on and be a success in life so that you can afford to buy the over priced tickets. And go on home and hug your parents. They deserve one for what you've put them through. Enjoy the rest of your Saturday. At least the sun hasn't gone down yet. Class dismissed.

FORWARD: PARENTING LECTURE

It has been my pleasure to have been a teacher in various capacities for what seems like the last eighty years. I have taught elementary school for five years, exceptional education with teenagers for sixteen years. I have had a hand in developing an academy for a school district, where we accept children that are expelled from the school system and try to turn their lives around. I have been the acting discipline coordinator for the same school system. In that capacity I would find myself sitting in a juvenile courtroom every Thursday, student records in my lap, watching my children go to jail. They were all good kids, but they all had done really bad things. And most of them came from families so dysfunctional that they didn't stand a chance at home, in school, in the courtroom, or in society. They were not bad families. These were not evil people; they just didn't possess one shred of any kind of proper parenting tools. When mom shows up in court with her bedroom slippers on, curlers in her hair, standing next to her son whose underwear is showing from underneath his "cocaine is the breakfast of champions" T-shirt, this is not a good sign. They need help. Their children need help. Locking a child in a cage is not help. It may be necessary for society, but it does not go under the heading of helpful services. It is my hope that this lecture, as lightweight as it is, will be of service to somebody, somewhere. The question is, how do you create children that can succeed in school and in life?

While most schools are wonderful places for children to be, staffed by true heroes in our society, I realize full well that a lot of schoolwork is dull; some teachers couldn't teach their way out of a paper bag and some administrators shouldn't be in charge of a pet, much less a student. This being said, I have also found that if a child is seriously struggling in school and exhibiting behavioral problems, which often go hand in hand, that there is often a child rearing struggle in the background that greatly magnifies whatever shortcomings that could be found in the school. The good news is that you can prepare your child for a successful life, NO MATTER WHAT KIND OF SCHOOL HE ATTENDS.

The secret of a child's success in school is what happens to them from conception to five years old. I do not like to use terms like "properly" when talking about child rearing, because they carry the baggage of moral judgement. Lord only knows there is enough judgement of child rearing practices, or lack there of, to go around. And around again. I will say that a five year old raised effectively is light years ahead of one raised ineffectively and is already miles down the road to success where the other child is still trying to find his driveway. The main thrust of this lecture is that no matter what the child's background, race, creed, color, religious affiliation, political party, gender, hairstyle or solar system they come from they can ALL succeed in school and in life if they are groomed for success. This is a child success grooming talk. Regardless of what kind of school your child goes to, YOU hold the keys to their success. Think about that for awhile before you jump for joy.

Being the key holder is liberating and scary at the same time. Professor Johnson is here to help with the liberating part and evaporate the scary part. Child rearing has been going on for thousands of years. It is not rocket science. What makes child rearing scary these days is not the child or the rearing. It's the *"these days"* that we're all having a problem with, parents and teachers alike. Welcome to the brave new world of raising successful children. This lecture serves as a roadmap. At least my publisher hopes so. She's counting on it, even as she eyes me warily.

Bill Hoatson

PROFESSOR JOHNSON'S INFAMOUS LECTURE ON PARENTING:

or

How to raise your child to be a success in life instead of headed for jail or a violent, possibly drug-addled death.

Preface

Professor Johnson's lecture on parenting - for - success was given at an In-House Suspension Room at Barkley High School in the spring of 2004. All of the students in attendance were there as part of their court-ordered rehabilitation program for sexually active, underage teenagers.

It is a pleasure to be here at Barkley High on a Saturday morning, even if this is the indoor suspension room. Some of my best lectures have been in ISS rooms. There's nothing like a captive audience. Now, if I look at my note card correctly, I see that we are here to talk about sex today. What a great way to start out a Saturday!

Usually, my talks are given to groups of students who deal with their problems by beating people up. The only time sex comes into the discussion is when we get to the part about life in prison. That is, if you call dead silence a discussion. So it's great to be amongst a bunch of young people who don't want to hurt anybody, they just want to get their groove on. Young lady, how old are you?.....16?........Young lady, how old are you?...... 14?...... Young man?.....15? Young man?..... 15? Let me ask you something. Do you think sex is natural or unnatural?..... How about you?......Young lady, would you characterize sex as fun or not fun?...... How about you?..... Did you realize there was a study done that shows how often your average human being has some kind of a sexual thought? For males its like once every thirty seconds, or some such crazy number. To sum up, sex is natural, it's fun as all get out, and everybody thinks about it all the time. On top of this, we live in a society where, I don't care what you're selling, there's an underclothed woman somewhere nearby. So, you are locked up on this beautiful Saturday morning for what? For being human? I say this is an outrage! This is an injustice.

What were they thinking about? I shall call the principal first thing Monday morning and give him a piece of my mind. Class dismissed. Let's go home.

Wait. Wait a minute. Please return to your seats. I almost forgot something. Thank you. I forgot to introduce a couple of very important visitors. Mrs. Wilson, could you please send your daughter up here, while I sit for a second?.......What's your name sweetheart?.....Shonterica? That's a beautiful name. Your parents have imagination. My name is Bill. How old are you?....4? What's your favorite food?. Chicken?Mine, too. What time is dinner?.....What do you mean you don't know? It's when I get there is when. Why don't you sit in my lap for a second? Now, Mrs. Woodbury, would you escort your reluctant son up here please? Hi, there young man. What's your name?..... I can't hear you while your face is in your mother's dress..... Robert? A very manly name. How old are you, Robert? Hold them up high and let me count. One, two, three. Three years old and no gray hair yet. How do you do it? And what is your favorite food? ....What's that? I can't quite make it out, but I think he said get me away from this crazy man before I cry. I want to thank you, Shonterica and Robert, for visiting me for a minute. It was a joy. Let's give them a round of applause, please. Thank you, Mrs. Williams, Mrs. Woodbury, for coming this morning. Bye.

You know, it dawned upon me that you're not in this room, on a Saturday, because of your interest in sex. You are here because of Shonterica and Robert...... Of course having two little children here was a set up. Let's call it a visual aid. Weren't they cool? Nothing cuter than a little child, if only they'd stay that way. You are here because of a large societal fear that if you have a Shonterica or a Robert, and are too immature to raise them properly, terrible things can happen to them. Did you see little Robert there, clinging to his mother? That child is totally dependent on her. The power that mother has over her child is terrifying. She can do anything to that child that she wants. She could beat him, starve him, abuse him, yell at him, lock him in a closet, torture him, neglect him, kill him. It's easy. There is not one single thing that child could do about it. As a parent, you have total power over another human being.

  I remember being married – way too young, by the way - living in a crowded trailer park, which is what happens when you get married way too young, because you don't have any money. I was surrounded by young couples in the same circumstances, except some had babies. I remember this young man shrieking at his baby each night, cursing at it, trying desperately to make it stop crying. Then there were the sounds of him beating the baby. I cried myself to sleep for two nights before I got up the courage to call the police.

  I don't know if the young man was evil or mentally ill. I have the horrible feeling that he was normal, except crushed by the weight of the awesome responsibility of caring for a human being, for which he was totally unprepared. Years later I do remember seeing my own infant son laying propped up on some pillows and almost fainting from the sheer magnitude of the responsibility and the overwhelming feeling of helplessness, both his and mine.

So, in the end, it is society's knowledge and fear of bad parenting that drives many of the sex laws between consenting, but also UNDERAGE people, meaning in your case, children. Now, I understand full well that many of you will have sex, no matter what I say. I could easily spend an hour on the hundred and one ways to PREVENT pregnancy. The fact is, you DO need to listen to that lecture, and listen carefully. I have found, however, that the best way to prevent pregnancy is to understand the enormity of the job of parenting. THAT understanding will not only drive you to go to a lecture on pregnancy prevention, but sit bolt-upright through it, because you are actually paying close attention. So I am going to conduct a class on parenting today. You're stuck with me for two hours, so you might as well get something out of it.

I have four goals in mind. One, is to instill in you the seriousness of child rearing so that it might change your reckless sexual behavior. Two, is to create a conceptual framework to work from so that you are not driven by fear or ignorance to do crazy things to your own child. Three, is to give you the tools to help create a glorious adulthood for your child. If done right, you can give your child a large head start on being a success in life. It is my firm belief that all children have great destinies. It is your job as parent to set the stage for their greatness. And, four, is to have a little fun. I don't see this as a wasted Saturday. This could be the best Saturday of your life…..What are you moaning about? By your behavior you were begging for a parenting class. Well, ask and ye shall receive. What a miraculous world we live in! You can just be thankful that this isn't a

Lamaze class.

Now, to begin. I brought several charts with me today. The first over here is the title of my lecture: "How to Raise Your Child to be a Success in Life Instead of Being Headed for Jail or a Violent, Possibly Drug-Addled, Death." Catchy, huh? Next is a list of the fifteen topics we'll cover.

Since sex is where it all begins, that's where we'll start. Rule number one is, parenting is for responsible adults only. A child cannot raise a child properly. Half of the adults out there can't either. It is the single hardest thing you'll ever do in your life.If you asked the man who conquered Mount Everest what his greatest feat was, he would not even mention anything that had to do with mountains, unless it was the mountain of debt he had accumulated for the college fund. Child rearing is deeply rewarding at times, but if anybody ever describes child rearing as fun, head for the exit, because the person is deeply disturbed, and possibly dangerous.

Now, I know you think you're grown. It is not your body that society is worried about, however. It's your brain. Are you capable of making adult choices? The short answer is ARE YOU KIDDING ME? Every brain has a corpus callosum. When it connects both sides of the brain it creates an organ capable of higher order, or adult thinking. The problem is, this doesn't happen until between 17 and 22 years old. Ever see one of your bright, intelligent friends do something really stupid? And you're going, "what was he thinking about?" Who knows? To the immature brain it seemed like a really cool idea at the time. Looking back at their own childhood, most adults are just happy to be alive, much less be a success. So society has passed laws that will put you in jail for having sex under18, because they KNOW you are not ready for parenthood. It's like giving a driver's license to a ten year old. The fact that he's big for his age and his foot reaches the peddle is besides the point.

Now, my own personal opinion is, if you're not ready to raise a child properly, you are not ready for sex. I don't care what age you are. A clue is if you engage in child thinking vs. adult thinking. The number one indicator is how self-centered you are. An infant is completely and totally self-centered. I'm hungry, I'm tired, I want, I, I, I. An adult factors in others and asks different questions, such as are you hungry?, are you tired?, what can I do for you? Don't ever have a birthday party catered by two year olds. You will go home not having had any fun and hungry, because they will share NOTHING with the guests. You should check your own self-centered meter. I had a pregnant student who had her meter stuck way over on "I." She was telling her girlfriends that her grandmother was going to raise her child for her so that she could achieve her life's goal: to go to the club and party a lot. I also give a separate lecture on what to do when grandma goes off the deep end and agrees, but that's for another time.

More subtly, I had a long, rather enlightening conversation with a young man, who was soon to be a dad. He talked about getting his child the finest things in life. He told me that if his boy wanted a $200 pair of shoes he would steal them for him if he had to. I asked him why, and he told me that his kid deserved as much as any rich kid. I admired that attitude, but asked him, what if you went to jail in the process? He said that he didn't care if he went to jail for ten years, his child was going to have the best. I let that sit for a moment and then I asked him if he really thought that his child would rather have a pair of shoes, or even gold or diamonds, than his own father? Sadly, his idea of fatherhood remained with giving things. The truth is, what a child wants and needs is you. Your love, your TIME. And lots of it. That's why its so hard for a lot of people to be good parents. *You can't just give your way to good parenthood.* The question becomes, are you and your partner willing to be on duty, 24/7, for the next 18 years of your life, not that you even really know what happens in 18 years of life. And in that 24/7 duty time, willing to devote large chunks of it to actually being with your child.

You noticed that I mentioned the word partner? Don't think for 30 seconds that you don't need one. Let's take a look at the next chart, which is the sex and money chart. Doesn't get much better than this in America, does it? Sex and money. I want you to take special note of this line here, which is taking a 75 degree nose dive into the ground. That's the single parent poverty death spiral. This 90 degree plunging line over here is the single parent with no diploma suicide drop. And this next chart, here, shows the number of young men under 20 who are willing to get married and stick with their sex partner once she becomes pregnant. ......What's that? ....Yes, I know that it's blank. Young men, I want you to look around the room and notice that you are the only ones laughing. Ladies, you know that frosty look you just gave Mr. Happy sitting next to you? You might want to use that a little more when they're throwing whatever passes for charm these days your way. Eighty-five percent of all households in poverty are headed by single parent women. This partner thing is huge and impacts the children in hundreds of different ways.

What happens when there is a pregnancy? You have three options. You and your partner can do whatever it takes to flip your self-centered needle way over to the adult side, act as a team, and set about the business of successful child rearing. This leads directly to our next topic, which is prenatal care.

Or, men, you can run and pretend you don't have a child. You can pretend like you don't even know the mother, couldn't pick her out of a police lineup. But in reality that pretend family of yours is going to go into the tank, and it's all your fault, and you know it.

What separates the men from the boys and the women from the girls is not the sex act. Any fool, if lucky enough, can do that. It's how you react to the word pregnant. Wishful thinking, pretending and running away are all highly valued tools that a child uses to deal with reality, but are the kiss of death to an adult. Which side do you fall on? If you fall on the adult side, let's start looking at the concrete steps for creating a successful child, from the day after "honey, I'm pregnant!" If you fall on the child side and feel completely overwhelmed, and unequipped to deal with having a child, there are lot's of agencies set up to help. Go to them. That's what they are there for. That is option three.

The building of a successful child starts from day one of the pregnancy. And the strength of the team will be tested one minute after that. That's right guys, you don't have 9 months to sit around and decide if you're joining the team or not. The team is hitting the field NOW. Job one for each team member is to answer the question "do I want this child?" This step is crucial, because the phrase "honey, I'm pregnant" does not always result in squeals of delight. This and the bankruptcy thing are the two real team killers. If you don't know the answer, go join Superman in his fortress of solitude, and don't come out until you do. Do whatever mental gymnastics it takes, because if the child is not wanted then you are not going to be willing to make the sacrifices necessary to raise a child properly. The baby does not care in the least if it is planned. It has a huge interest in being loved and wanted, however. If you can get to where you can say, "I want the baby" in the mirror and keep a straight face without the support of a Jack Daniels bottle, then you are halfway home to being a good parent. The rest of this will be as easy as drinking water.

Now begins the prenatal care phase: raising a child for success inside the mother's body. First, let's look at the next chart. This is fascinating. It shows the different stages of fetal development in the womb, every six weeks. You can see the skeletal development, lung development. Over here is enormous brain development.

A couple rules of thumb. The fetus is part of mom, directly attached to mom through the umbilical cord. Whatever mom eats, fetus eats. Mom drinks, fetus drinks. Mom breathes, fetus breathes. See your doctor about what is best to eat, drink and breathe.

The proper diet during the proper six weeks time frame will go a long way to having a child with a properly developed brain that will function efficiently at school. You are now building a college graduate.

I used the word sacrifice a little while ago and saw some of you squirm in your seats. If you think sacrifice is a curse word then that should tell you something about yourself. It means the needle on your self-centered meter is way over to the left, stuck in child mode. There is nothing wrong with that, per se, just don't risk having children by having sex.

So here come the sacrifices. Ladies, no alcohol, cigarettes, drugs, junk food, violence or anger during pregnancy. Eat properly, take your vitamins, see your doctor, and get plenty of sleep. You with me on this? Sometimes it helps to actually hang this chart on a wall somewhere in your house so that you can visually see why you're doing without all this stuff that you should be doing without anyway. It helps your determination. Men, you can help your partner greatly with this by following the same rules. What do you mean WHAT? You think it helps your team mate, who is chewing on the furniture to alleviate her tobacco cravings, to look outside and see you blowing smoke rings out in the front yard. "Hey baby, you want a cold one?" and you throw her a pineapple juice while you pull the tab on a tall Budweiser. No, Buddy-Ro, that's not going to fly. Young lady, pass this bag back to the father-to-be in purple. It looks like he's going to be sick. What's that?.....I hear you. I don't blame you. Yes, sir?..... While the abortion option is there, my only reaction to that is that's easy for a man to say. Plus, we're talking about successful child rearing practices today, so we're assuming that there actually is a child to practice on. Whew, sex is serious business. We might as well stay serious for a couple of more minutes. Back to the chart: young lady, let's say your are a heroin addict and have got to shoot up. GOT to. Which six weeks period would you pick to do the least harm?..... What do you mean it's a lousy choice? Of course it's a lousy choice. I had a girl one time say in the first six weeks, because there was less to mess up. As you correctly deduced by looking at the chart, there is no optimum time for destroying your child.

    I have taught for almost 30 years, many of which were spent with children with learning or behavioral disabilities. Do not set your child up for a lifetime of being in the principal's office explaining why he was terrorizing the classroom when, in fact, he couldn't sit still if he wanted to because his entire central nervous system was rewired due to massive amounts of drugs or alcohol. Set your child up for success instead, with good prenatal care. Once the child is born, he's now got a great foundation to grow from: he's loved, and he's healthy, and he's born into a focused, functioning, FAMILY UNIT for support.

    Now that you actually have a child, the next step is nutrition. Again..... Yes, ma'am, what's that?.....What are we doing? This is a new concept. It is called planning for the future. Even better, proactively shaping the future. It's the vision thing, which, if I'm not mistaken, is number two on the list separating adult thinking from child thinking.....This makes your head hurt? Well, the learning process is prone to doing that every once in a while. Just watch.

You'll love this. I'll show you how to raise a genius just by shopping. Well, don't get too excited. I'm talking about grocery shopping.

In order for a body and a brain to function properly it must get the right nutrients. Sounds simple enough. A person needs to be fed. The problem is, half of the food in the grocery store is not food, in any real sense of the word. I have never seen a country with so much wealth that people don't eat for survival, but for entertainment. I can see a guy from Bangladesh talking to a U.S. citizen: "What are you eating?" "Just junk. They call it junk food." "Oh, I'm so sorry. I didn't realize it was so bad over here." "No, that's ok. I eat this on purpose." "Oh, do you now?", he says as he slowly backs away from the deranged American. Let's put this into an equation. Junk food equals junk brain, and junk body, which equals fat, bloated, idiot death. The real axis of evil is sugar, grease and salt. Some genius figured out how to take the cheapest commodities on the planet and turn them into gold. You can not grow one single brain cell with sugar, grease, or salt. Earth to mom and dad. You are not feeding your child for amusement sake only. Building a good brain and body better factor in there somewhere. If you start early, it's easy. My daughter avoids sugar laden cereal because, starting around two years old, I would walk her up and down the cereal aisle and tell the story of the soulless corporate billionaire. This man's sole purpose in life was to make lot's of money. He didn't have the spine to be a crack dealer nor the stomach to be a hit man, so he settled on selling chocolate donut cereal to helpless children instead. If they would sell sugar and fat laden products to children to bilk their parents out of their money before their child dies, what else are they capable of doing? Are there no limits to their depravity and greed? Variations of this little fable also works wonders in the snack food aisle or your local "music" store.

Your average child, after getting this over the top response from parent EVERY TIME they ask for something harmful, will not ask anymore. "Put that garbage back on the shelf quick, before dad sees you. Don't get him started!" After awhile, they won't even think about asking, which is exactly what you want. Get the stuff off their radar screen.

It "tastes good" or it's "nasty" has a lot more to do with what a child is used to than how food actually tastes. I have seen children dump trays full of good meals, calling it "nasty" and then eating chips or candy bars the rest of the day. Your first line of defense is your home. The first few years of life give you a chance to set up habits that will last your child a lifetime. This difference between "nasty" or "good" is simply what a child has experienced..

A good place to start is NEVER use sugar or candy as a reward for ANYTHING. Don't have any junk food inside your house. When the child opens the refrigerator she sees applesauce, fruits, carrot sticks, yogurt, whole grain breads and peanut butter. Whatever. These are the treats they run for, because that's all there is. And if you treat them like treats they become treats, especially if you actually use the word "treat" when handing it to them. Once you form a habit of eating right, it will stick, or at least be there to fall back on later in life.

I know this is sacrilege, but sodas, candy and chips are not food. If you were left on an island with only sodas, candy and chips the rescue team three years later would find a 300 pound dead person with a misspelled plea for help next to him. And I'm willing to bet that he was hyperactive right up to the bitter end. I am not going to beat this nutrition thing to death, but it is crucial when you are building a child for success that you use the right materials. And food is one of the few things that you can actually control, at least at home. You can build a car using plastic and cardboard, I suppose, just don't expect it to run efficiently or last very long. Here's a little ditty you can remember for vegetables: something orange, something green, your brain percolates like a well oiled computing machine; only sugar, only something sweet, that shrunk up little brain will have to take a back seat, it can't compete, it can't perform an intelligent feat…..Thank you for the applause, but why don't we save it for the dirty jokes at the end.

OK. We've now got a real, live child who is loved and healthy. We are going to get very specific on what a parent can do to facilitate the big three: language, reading and math. We'll take language first. Language rule one: the more quantity of words that a child hears from birth to four, the more you are building a child's brain for language and reading ability. You have permission to drink lots of coffee and chatter away like a magpie in an amphetamine lab. Talk to and around your child a lot, from day one. It doesn't matter in the least that your child doesn't respond and you feel like a fool. The more the better. If you are a frustrated actor, writer, or stand-up comic, let it out. Stand at the crib and do Shakespeare. Try out your rotten comedy routines as you change out a diaper. The worst you'll get are smiles and goo-goos, which is a heck of a lot better than the usual reaction you'll get from drunken adults at nightclubs.

Shut up is not a conversation. If you are unloved, overworked, underpaid, undervalued, unhealthy, trapped in a lousy relationship, or just plain mean: in other words, if your life is so stressed that the least little thing sets you off, get a pet instead of a child. And don't go for the dog, because they require way too much work. Start with a goldfish.

Shut up! Be quiet! I don't want to hear a sound! Well, Mr. I wish my child was a rock instead of a human being, you should have thought of that before you decided to get your freak on. Lot's of language, in a normal tone of voice is important for the brain. Yelling and screaming don't count.

Besides quantity, variety is important. The more different words that a child hears from birth, the more complex brain development you will get. If I were to take the top off of an adult's head and took the brain out, what would it look like?..... A squiggly mess? That's exactly correct. And the more squiggles the better because they are learning and retrieving informational paths. A newborn's brain is fairly smooth. What you don't want is a 16 year old to have the brain wrinkles of a billiard ball. So build vocabulary. Take the stroller up to a flower and start naming the parts. Ignore the fact that all your child really can do is drool well. Go for it. If you don't know anything your own self, drag a dictionary around with you. That's what I do. When you see somebody coming, bend over and say, "I am going to circumvent the corrosive effects of profane language upon your intellect by heaping voluminous amounts of positive adjectives on your little brilliant head". Which will elicit the usual "What?" from your limited vocabulary friends. Occasionally, you will have a friend whose vocabulary is not so limited, who will answer, "What the bleep!" instead. Let's talk profanity for a minute. This language acquisition thing is great, but there are certain words that you don't want your child to acquire. These, unfortunately, are the ones that are picked up in a millisecond. You can work on the word symphony all you want, but if the child hears the word "bleep", that's all you're going to get. If you're lucky you might get, "Boy, that was a great bleeping symphony." Nowadays, however, it's not just your mouth or your friend's mouth that you have to watch out for. There is an entire industry making millions off of turning your child into a disrespectful, criminal, moron. Don't play this "musical entertainment" around them. A hint is if the title has the word "nasty" in it, like "You're Momma's Got a Nasty New Boyfriend", or "Big Nasty Booty". These are not children's songs on the par of "It's a Small World After All". Now, before you get on your high horse, I'm not telling you what to do. I'm telling you what to do around your child. Big and important difference. Your days of thinking about just number one are just about over. If you look closely, the number one is now on a t-shirt being worn by your child, number two is on your spouses shirt, numbers three through eight are on other family members and nine through fifteen belong to colleagues at work. Welcome to the adult world. You're lucky if your shirt has a number in double digits.

If you have given your child the proper foundation for language skills: quantity, quality, and variety, the foundation is also laid for reading, WHICH IS THE SINGLE MOST IMPORTANT SINGLE SKILL THAT A CHILD MAY HAVE. It is also relatively easy to impart, as are most skills if you have the one, single attribute besides love that separates all good parents and teachers from the mediocre: that is patience. If you don't have any, go to the store and buy some, because you're going to need it. Buy it in the giant, economy sized pack.

How fascinating is it, exactly, to sound out d…..o……g…….dog, for the 48th time? To write the letter "o" over and over again, until done properly? Your child needs you to have the capacity to be bored out of your mind and not show it. You can't fidget, look exasperated, or get angry, because the little brain that is apparently processing information slower than the garden slug that it was inspecting earlier, is going as fast as it can. If you add fear or hostility into the mix, it will not only slow down, but stop. If you think you were frustrated at slow, you'll go ballistic at dead stop. Don't think of a child as a little human being, but as a little mule. What you don't want is for the mule to plant itself, braying for all the world to hear, and refuse to move. This is what you will get if you don't exhibit PATIENCE while a child is learning. There is a little town in Georgia that celebrates Mule Day every year. Well, it will be mule day around your house every day if you don't let learning happen at its natural pace, following its natural course.

What is the natural course? For reading, you simply place the child on your lap, starting with the ride home from the hospital, and read a book. Every night. THAT'S ALL. *It does not take a rocket scientist to teach reading. It takes time and patience. The child's brain is naturally going to absorb the process.* It will figure out that in America, we read from left to right and top to bottom. That we turn pages. That letters make sounds. That a period is a stop sign. That reading is enjoyable. As the baby gets a little older, you start pointing out what sounds each letter makes, or each blend. You point to key words like "cat" or "jump", and have the child read the whole word. After a few years – the patience thing – the child is reading to YOU. And this is all before a child enters school. They will not only be school ready, but set up to excel in it.

DO NOT EXPECT THE SCHOOL TO TEACH YOUR CHILD TO READ. If you wait until school age to introduce your child to reading, your child is already five years behind everybody else when he enters school and will struggle his whole life to catch up. I cannot stress this enough. A teacher with a one-to-twenty ratio, at best, is not able to do what a parent, who is one-on-one, can do with a child. Not even close. And it's not their job to fill a five year void, because while they're doing that, the child is missing what he currently should be getting.

You, as parent, can ensure your child's success. That is the good news. When they are very young get the baby cloth books, which are made for chewing on. Then let them chew it and enjoy the book. Help them make their own books as they get older. They love this. They get to use paper, staplers, glue, crayons, rulers, pencils, pens, markers, computers, whatever. They also get to do the artwork and book format. Being an author of a book, even one that only has three words on each page, is an empowering thing for a child. It is the joy of reading times two, because it adds the element of performance to it, with adult approval as a reward, which is a giant incentive. Let them read their books to you, their grandmother, the traveling salesperson that you are trying to get rid of. It doesn't matter. *The adult approval that they will receive for their intellectual abilities is worth its weight in gold. The child feels that his power base is centered in his brain. This is exactly where you want your child to feel powerful, because there are a lot of negative power sources,* which we'll discuss later. I once ran a behavioral class for violent 4th and 5th graders. Most were reading on a kindergarten or first grade level. We would make our own books and learn to read them. If they behaved themselves that day their reward was to walk down to the office and read out loud to the principal, secretary, janitor or any willing adult that they could rustle up. It was like magic. These children would do ANYTHING to stay out of trouble so that they could go show off their reading. It was the highlight of their day. It was definitely the highlight of the adult's day to watch these children beaming with pride at their intellectual accomplishments. This was the raw power of positive attention at its best. *I have found that if children get enough positive attention then they won't spend their energy doing outrageous things to get your attention in a negative way.* The bottom line is, they are going to get attention one way or the other. Which do you prefer? The beauty of giving and getting positive attention for reading is that after awhile it becomes a self-generating positive energy machine, because the act of reading itself is so rewarding on its own. It is also the one intellectual gift, if you had only one to give, that will help your child succeed in life above all others. So give it. It is yours to give. Just make sure that the child is having fun with words. And that you and other adults are part of that fun.

Give books as gifts and make a big deal out of getting one. Give reading in the disguise of games, like crossword puzzles and spelling dice. When they get older, have a family reading time of at least one half hour, where they read for pleasure every day. Read books yourself and let junior see you do it. This is critical and, judging by the moaning and groaning, means another radical lifestyle change for some of you.

I'm going to give you an insight into parenting that will last you a lifetime. The secret is that no child wants to be a child. They all want to be grown. The only people who actually want to be children are adults. They have seen both sides of the equation and have figured that children, by far, have the better deal. Children have not seen both sides of the equation yet, so they spend all their efforts towards what they see as the better deal: being a grown-up.

There is one powerful phrase that a parent needs to keep in the fore part of their mind. It is also my entire drug lecture, which I'll give right now: MONKEY SEE, MONKEY DO. That explains everything. That's it. If you want your child to read, you read. If you want her to be a profanity spewing, ax wielding alcoholic, then that is what you model. A family reunion would be a perfect time for this. Children spend their whole life aspiring to be you, to be an adult.

The power of the parent to shape a child, for good or bad, is awesome, even to an adult in their forties. It is overwhelming for one who is too young, particularly because parenting has a lot to do with YOU and how YOU conduct yourself. If you are not willing to make personal changes for the betterment of another human being, then don't put yourself in the position of being a parent. In case any of this sounds familiar, you may consider it a THEME, which may come in handy if you have to write a paper on this for school.

You've prepared your child for language use and reading. Now it's math time. A lot of math tasks stimulate a different part of the brain than reading tasks, so we need to do different preps than the reading and language preps. One thing as a parent is real easy. Get your child a bunch of blocks and let them play. Building things with their hands develops a certain spatial sense, which is half of what higher math is anyway.

Small children need a sense of one-to-one correspondence. Ask your child how many chairs are in the room, and have them touch the chair as they are counting. Kids love this. Children learn through touching. Their need to touch is somewhat akin to that of Uncle Fred's tobacco need when he is out of cigarettes. It is an absolute necessity. Don't have the mentality of the owner of an expensive antique store in your house. On this note, you do realize that you are going to have to child-proof your entire house, which means barring the doors to everything dangerous and placing everything else at least ten feet off the ground. Once the child learns to crawl, it's fifteen feet.

Play spatial games, such as dot-to-dot, checkers, or chess. Have them do puzzles. Play dice games. Play anything that has numbers in it. Dust off the old roulette wheel and see how he does. This could be useful later in case the college thing doesn't go so well. There are a ton of ways a simple BINGO set up can be used.

Give a small earned allowance to instill knowledge of money. As the child gets older, realistic money based problems are a motivator for learning proper math skills, like "I don't have any idea where you are going to get fifty bucks, but your date will be here in ten minutes." Money and math are one and the same. One peaks a lot more interest than the other, though, so go with the money to get math principals across. Playing store is a hoot. Keep empty boxes and a calculator around. Playing store can kill half of a rainy Saturday, especially if you add the rules about being thrown out of the store if the proper store etiquette isn't followed. There is nothing more joyful as the look on a child's face as he pitches the adult from his doorstep for not saying "please." Keeping a mock checking account is also a blast. You can get all the blank checking account ledgers you want from your nearest bank. Hear your child shriek with glee as the bank teller gets to call security because they found errors on your deposit slip.

Fractions can be taught through hands-on tasks. Cut paper to specified lengths. Pretend like it's expensive walnut and watch their little faces drop when they are docked a weeks pay for miscutting an expensive "board". This will get you even for being handcuffed at the bank. Percentages are easy to explain if you use the criminal nature of the credit card process as an example.

You noticed that I mentioned the word "play" a lot. Play is how a child learns. There is no differentiation between work and play. Only adults separate the two. Get a child a toy vacuum cleaner or lawn mower for a present, they think it's great. Grown-ups are less cheery about it, because it signifies work, which is the adult version of a four letter word. The child's brain will absorb things quickly if they are put into a game form. And you can make a game out of anything. Instead of showing a flash card and saying "this is a five" you can have a treasure hunt for numbers and hide them around the kitchen. You can test gravity by dropping items from a high place, such as water balloons on an older brother. Science is a riot. Science is a good excuse to work on your math skills. And science is easy because science is anything you say it is. It is jello going from a liquid to a solid state. It is checking how many miles per gallon your family car gets and comparing it to the nitwit down the street who just bought a Sherman Tank for carrying groceries. It is a magnifying glass in a child's hand. Shoot, just buy a globe and let your child play with it. You'll be amazed how fast they can find the capitol of Zimbabwe while you're still trying to locate the proper continent. And if you can't find a way to make games involving science you need to check your pulse. It may be time to give the crematorium a heads up.

During any game you are accomplishing four

things: spending time with your children, which is love and bonding, having fun, imparting knowledge, and getting out of chores. "Honey, would you mow the lawn, please?" "I can't right now, because I'm playing with our precious daughter. You should see how much she is learning." This playing with the child thing is a stroke of genius. You even have a built in excuse to see every child movie ever made. There is no downside to playing. So why are some schools set up like misery factories that kids trudge off to everyday? You need to write your local legislator and ask, because I don't have a clue. But it doesn't have to be like that in your house.

Keep in mind two things. One, is that the brain absorbs information easily and naturally. That is what it does, just as the stomach digests food. The other is that ANYTHING can be ruined if forced. A child learns to master language all by himself. If you decide to force the issue, shrieking "not dadda, ….. DADDY, DADDY" at him, you can create all kinds of speech problems not to mention the lifelong fear of DADDY. I've seen all kinds of eating disorders created by harsh, mean commands at the dinner table. Sex itself can be ruined if it is unpleasant. I've seen kids grow up hating to read or hating science. How is that even possible? It's like hating to talk. If you say things like "I said E, not E flat – E! What's the matter with you?" I can guarantee you that that child is not going to race upstairs to practice his violin during his spare time. Now, he may offer it up if a little more kindling is needed for the campfire.

So make your house a safe, fun place to learn, which leads to one last word on games. I DON'T mean competition where you have winners and losers. I mean setting up learning in a non-work atmosphere. You don't want to be prancing around the room like Mohammed Ali after beating your child in a number game while he is wailing inconsolably in the bathroom. Each child's competition lust is different and arrives at different stages in life. Let them dictate any competition. In small children, the possibility of LOSING at something often negates any possible fun and short-circuits the learning because the child is focused on not being publicly humiliated. Have fun without it. There is no such thing as a loser in learning. If you must compete have it be you and your child against a goal, or the child striving to beat his own standard.

    We need to talk about the effects of TV on your child's brain sometime, and now seems as good a time as any. The power of learning through play is that the child is interacting with his environment. He is touching, smelling, tasting. Better yet, he might be interacting with other people. It is through the physical interaction with their environment that a young child learns. The actual process of watching TV is the exact opposite of the learning process. Instead of being active, you are passive and the only environment you come into contact with is the couch. And you can't interact with people because you are constantly telling them to shut up and stop interrupting your show. I don't care how high the quality of the show is, the act of watching television is anti-learning. See this chart here? This is an eye opener. If you will notice, this rising line here, which represents hours of watching TV per day, correlates perfectly with this descending line here, which is a child's shrinking grade point average. It doesn't get any plainer than that. When you watch TV, within minutes your brainwaves go from an active pattern to something between hypnosis and sleep. Some people call it the electronic fireplace. Before TV, people used to stare at fires, which is also hypnotic. Now, if you've had a hard day at work and feel the need to come home and be entertained, which in the case of TV is hypnosis with a theme, there is absolutely nothing wrong with that. Join the club. It's a big one. But the effects on children, who should be DOING SOMETHING instead of just sitting there staring, are devastating. Why would a parent plunk their child down in front of the zombie machine for hours everyday? Because they're wicked? Sick? Twisted? How about just plain tired? Or wore out? They need a break from real life, which is work and parenting. …..Oh, I see. Well, the reason why you're not worn out is that you don't have any children yet. I can give a seventeen year old powerhouse a set of twins and come back six weeks later and he's been replaced by a tired, stooped, eighty year old man with a cranky disposition. Shoot, the reason why I'm here giving you this lecture is that I'm TRYING TO SAVE YOU'RE LIFE. At least life as you know it now. The fact is that many adults are too tired for their own children. We ALL have to guard against the natural tendency to use the television as a babysitter. Set up some rules about TV, made before you are too tired to think, or it will rule your house. It will swallow your child whole. I have visited many households of families whose children are struggling in school. I have seen households where the TV is on all day long. All night long. Multiple TV's. There isn't a place in the house where you could have a normal conversation, much less a quiet space to have a real thought. A child should not watch much TV or computer screens at all before the age of four. After that, limit viewing to an hour or two per day, if, behaviorally and scholastically, they have earned it. Make sure that they are getting enough of what they really need, such as play, exploration, reading, conversation, etc. A little TV watching is not going to hurt anybody. The code word is "little", which means DO NOT buy a TV for your child's bedroom. I am going to jump ahead real quick to parent discipline skills. Everybody, together. Say NO!….. NO WAY…..ARE YOU SERIOUS? …..NYET…..NEIN …..NON…..NOT…..NADDA….. Very good. Remember that, because it will also come in very handy when you are deciding, with your child, what shows they are actually allowed to watch.

You think the act of watching television is bad, what about the content? I had a kindergarten class once. It was St. Patrick's Day, so I figured that making a leprechaun would be a fitting project. When I mentioned it to the children, however, they reacted with horror and revulsion. It took me a couple of minutes to realize that some enterprising, young studio executive had recently made a movie about a diabolical, murderous leprechaun and of course, EVERY ONE of these five year olds had seen it, and now screech at the sight of anything Irish. If they can make a few more classics about murdering Santas and Easter Bunnies we can wipe out a lot of holidays, which would be a great stress reducer for adults. If you want to start a heated argument, go into your average second grade and ask who's badder, Freddy or Jason? Oh, you'll touch off something there, because they will all have an opinion, because they WILL ALL HAVE SEEN IT. Two thoughts spring immediately to mind. Where are the parents and why haven't they been kneecapped yet? Does anybody actually think that there is some kind of special soap or scrub brush out there that will erase horrible images from a child's mind? I even had a parent tell me one time that her eight year old wasn't effected by violent murder scenes. She said, no, it doesn't bother him, he just laughs at it. Now, let THAT sink in for a moment. Like, laughing while somebody is being stabbed to death is a superior response than crying and running, which is what normal people would do. Now, it is hard to talk to clueless parents, because they get very oversensitive about their ignorance, so it needs to be handled delicately. The technique that works for me is yelling WHAT WERE YOU THINKING ABOUT? at them while speed dialing 911. I mean, come on now. I can see the family sitting around, looking at the movie guide. "Let's see now, we can watch "Little Fluffy Finds a Home", "Brave Jeremy Saves an Entire Family", or "Sara Goes on a Blood Soaked Killing Spree". Well, that's a no brainer. Click. "Boy, that Sara sure is something, isn't she?" I mean, really. What ARE they thinking about? I am sure that the verb "thinking" does not apply here. Adults going through the motions of the day, surviving until the next day. I am not sure that a lot of adults appreciate the true beauty of a child, which is their sensitivity. I learned a large, unpleasant lesson once while watching TV with my daughter when she was seven. We were watching the Andy Griffith Show, which to me was a very safe, high quality show. Nothing to worry about here. Otis comes in drunk to lock himself in the cell, which is the gag. I am laughing away, even though I've seen the episode probably two hundred times, when I noticed that my daughter not only wasn't laughing, but had a disturbed look on her face. "What is that man doing?", she asked. Well, he's drunk and......" "What is drunk?" "Well, it's when somebody has had too much alcohol to drink and they get dizzy." "Why are you laughing, Daddy? I don't get it." All of a sudden I wasn't laughing anymore, in fact was feeling quite uncomfortable. I had seen this show over and over, but it had been a long, long time since I had seen it through a child's eyes. Explaining alcohol abuse as humor is impossible. The more I tried, the more uncomfortable I got and the more confused she got. I switched to the Cosby Show and just prayed that there were no wine jokes in it. As adults, we often forget how sensitive kids are, because we've seen and done way too much. That television experience with my daughter was a wake up call. If children can discern disturbing elements in even the most innocent settings, what does viewing full throttle violence do to their minds? *I suggest that you don't beat their sensitivity into callousness and indifference by pounding them with negative images. You are literally pounding the childhood right out of them.*

I am going to press three points here, all interrelated: the power of images, the role of violence in brain development, and the formation of a child's own self image. Images, once seen, can never be erased from the brain. Never. The brain may try its best to sublimate, or bury, certain unpleasant images, but they are still there. They can still be seen decades later. We have all seen unpleasant things. Conjure one up. See? They're still there. At my age I can still remember my younger brother getting sick all over the inside of my dad's car. Of course, that happened just last week, so I guess that doesn't count. As a parent, you have a responsibility and a duty to let your child be a child by shielding them from things that they should not see. I am talking mostly about violence and sex. There is absolutely no excuse for exposing your children to this. None. There are laws against it which are never enforced, but it is nevertheless criminal, because the effects are everlasting and serious. There have been several studies done on violence and children. A child immersed in violence has a brain that attends to information differently from one that isn't. Some kids stare at the blackboard to glean information, while others stare worriedly over their right shoulder to keep an eye on behavioral challenged classmates. If you find yourself living in a violent community it is especially important that you pull "Fluffy Finds a Home" off the shelf, because there has to be a mental safe harbor somewhere. Which child do you want to have in school? The one who is studiously caring for his plant in the science fair, experimenting on how the chlorophyll process can be adapted somehow for the betterment of mankind, or Jimmy The Thug, who is concentrating on how many of his boys he can talk into jumping on the young scientist who had accidentally brushed up against him in the hallway?

Violence is the enemy. The problem with violence is that it consumes all the air in the room. I don't care what is going on, violence has the ability to take it over and destroy it. You can be at the mall, a ball game, a doctor's office, or a classroom, and if a fight breaks out all normalcy in that situation is lost. All attention goes to the violence. All activity goes to it, either by stopping it, fueling it, or avoiding it. All conversation revolves around it, even for days after. Take a long look at a nine year old. How much has violence and his reaction to it taken over his brain? Does he attend to positives, academics, and construction, or negatives, violence, and destruction? Are his conversations mostly positive or negative? When I was in high school many of my conversations revolved around a girlfriend, real or imagined. Nowadays the conversation revolves around who is going to beat whom up, real or imagined. There is a lot of violence in the world these days. Do not throw gas on the fire by showing a child lots of negative images. Remember, all a child really wants to be is an adult. What kind of adult? Normal is whatever a child is surrounded by. Hate, fighting, yelling, or love, cooperation and respect are all normal to a child that knows nothing else. You are raising an adult when you are raising a child. What you get out of it is what you put into it. Monkey see, monkey do rules the world.

What is your own image of your child? Do you want your child to be productive and stay out of jail? Then don't let him see countless images that tell him that's exactly where he's going. Where, in fact, he belongs, as if he's got some kind of sacred jail destiny.

One day you will find things coming out of your

mouth that will sound eerily like whatever crazy thing your parents said to you when they were mad, like, WHO DO YOU THINK YOU ARE? That's the anti-disrespect response. The child is steady talking back to dad, telling dad what to do and what not to do. What you are going to get is "WHO DO THINK YOU ARE?", often followed by some kind of atomic explosion. And you know what? That is probably one of the most important questions that a parent can ask. Who DOES little Robert think he is? Everything this child does, good or bad, is related to his own self image. The power of outside images is that after awhile they get internalized. The outside becomes the inside, and once inside that child's own head and heart, what do you do? Teaching a child who thinks that he is stupid or bad is an entirely different ballgame than one who has a self view of being smart or good. If a child internalizes a negative view of himself it puts up huge barriers between him and his parents and teachers. Once that barrier is erected adults find themselves less and less trying to teach little Robert and more and more trying to save Robert from his own destructive tendencies.

What is a parent's image of their child? Some parents, and I'm one of them, firmly believe that a child can be anything he wants to be if he is willing to work hard for it. This belief is enormously important because if you believe it, the child will come to believe it. I find it to be absolutely true. A child's own belief system is going to shape their life. Like many things, this is a two edged sword. If they want to be a plumber or architect, that's fine. They may actually be helpful to you in your old age. But what if they want to be a criminal? I'll say that again. What if they REALLY think that they are going to be a criminal? What are you, as parent, going to do about it? Because they will meet their own perceived fate if you just stand there, staring in disbelief.

    I was mentoring a group of ninth graders once: the same group, once a week, all year long, so we had a good rapport with each other. Towards the end of the year I posed the question of how they saw themselves making money ten years into the future. The fact that most didn't even think they were going to live that long, much less PLAN for it should have been a hint that this might not go well. One at a time I wrote their ideas on the board. When it was done, we all sat back and looked at our collaboration. This is a true story, I swear it. We had written selling drugs, stealing, getting pregnant for the check, getting someone else pregnant for the check, just going to the mailbox and getting a check, winning the lottery, playing professional sports, or being a rap or music star. That's it. Period. Let me tell you something, you could hear a pin drop in that room when we were done. I wasn't shocked, but they sure were. They had never come face to face with the ugly reality that they carried around in their heads and hearts. Your own self image is something that you are not really aware of, it just slowly develops over time. It's like breathing. You don't notice it, but it's there and influences everything you do.

    So who DOES your child think he is? If you cannot see the posters of rock stars dressed all in black through the curtain of skulls that your teenager has put up, you might want to have a talk with him. If your child refers to you as my maid b... instead of mom it may be a sign to bring out the hammer, what a parent would call a CD equalizer. If your daughter wants to wear a G-string for Halloween and go as a video background star you may want to find a couple of minutes out of your busy day to have a little chat. If your son has his underwear showing 92% of the time, this tells you exactly how that child views himself. He's probably not modeling himself after a doctor.

A positive self - image is even more important for children with learning disabilities. All people, no matter what age, want to feel powerful, which really means having control over their life. Nobody desires to be helpless, living in a world where things just happen to you. And, if you are powerless, one senses that a lot of those things aren't going to be good.

Where does power come from? Many places, which can be a bit of a problem for human beings. It can come from the head: intellect, wit, academic ability, problem solving. It can come from the heart: compassion, empathy, charity. It can come from the body: physical prowess, agility, beauty. It can come from the soul: art, drama, music. These are all positive and productive.

But what if your child struggles in school and is made fun of? What if school is a place where they feel uncomfortable, inferior, helpless, powerless? What is that child going to do? Go to the other source of power, of course. A veritable fountain of power. Go to the DARK SIDE. Money, sex, violence. The shortcuts to success. Take Suzie. She can't read very well and math to her is like learning Chinese. Every time she tries to put pen to paper, it doesn't turn out so well. More like a seven year old than a seventeen year old. But put her in a thong bikini and men – not just boys, but grown men – would happily enter a point-blank shotgun contest just to spend five minutes with her. Now, where does she view her power source? Is it more likely that Suzie will become a leading cancer researcher or a pole dancer at Big Daddy's Fun Club?

Take Steven. He is laughed at all day at school. Thought per cent was cat money. Martin Luther King Jr. was president during the civil war. His science fair project was a stick. But at midnight he can make more money in an hour than a teacher earns in a month and just by whipping his gun out while growling like a preliterate Neanderthal can clear an entire parking lot in under five seconds. Where, exactly, does Steven think his power is coming from? Is it more likely that he will become a craftsman carpenter, or do ten to twenty at the state's Dude Ranch Gone Bad?

Students who are struggling at school, especially those with learning disabilities, are cannon fodder for people who make their money off of negative power sources. Shoot, there are millions of kids with absolutely no faith in their intellectual abilities to do anything positive. A giant army of Darth Vader wannabes marching to the thug-life drummer.

So, what is a parent to do? Get mad. Repeat after me, NOT MY CHILD…..Is that the best you can do? People are stealing your children. Come on gentlemen, everybody up. Now give me that power stance. You know how to do it. Give me the arms folded, head cocked, glaring thing. There you go.

Now let's use it for something more useful than terrorizing your grandmother into letting you stay out late. NOT MY CHILD…..NOT MY CHILD.

Now, parents-to-be, we're not helpless. Let's DO something. Let's use what we know to our advantage. *If a child feels the power of their intellectual ability, they are much less likely to go to the dark side for a power source.* Constantly praise and nurture intellectual ability. It is easy to fall into the old habits of telling a girl how pretty she is or a boy how strong he is. There is nothing wrong with that as long as you also add what a genius you think he or she is. Also, self - image develops early, so plan on planting positive images from birth. How you and your spouse conduct each other are the first images your child will internalize. Images are powerful. Use that power by being a positive role model and surround your child with pictures of positive role models. If your child is an Hispanic girl named Maria, some of the pictures in her house should be of Hispanic women doing positive things: doctor, pilot, scientist, brick mason. You don't have to lecture Maria in her crib about how all things are possible, because she will have grown up seeing it. When it becomes internalized, seeing it becomes believing it.

If you believe that something is possible, then in reality it becomes possible. Case in point: a famous black actor – I believe it was Will Smith, but my memory isn't what it once was-said that when he was young, seeing Ohura sitting at her station on the starship Enterprise while he was watching Star Trek opened all kinds of mental doors for him. Black people in positions of importance, as scientists, as

ACTORS. Once the mental door is opened it just becomes a matter of motivation to walk through it.

One of the best positive imaging posters of all time is next on this chart. This is from World War II. Women were desperately needed to work in munitions factories and other "male" jobs. Here is Rosie the Riveter, a woman showing her toughness in a typically male pose, flexing her muscles, with the words WE CAN DO IT emblazoned on it. How powerful is that? How many millions of girls and boys had their world view changed because of that image? How many millions of mental doors did this open up, especially at a time when, normally, if a sign were made with women in it, they would be standing in the middle of a kitchen?

The story of the four minute mile is illuminating. For years running a four minute mile was thought impossible. Not just real hard, but impossible. Until somebody broke it. Not too long after that the record was broken again, several times, because the mental block about it being impossible was gone. People had SEEN it beaten.

So put any kind of barrier busting pictures on the wall you want. They will open a floodgate of mental possibilities for your child. Black Nobel Prize winning scientists, female heavy equipment operators, male nurses, Chinese cowboys, the famous Jamaican bobsledders. And if you're putting pictures on the wall for boys, make sure most of the men are smiling. And gunless. I mean, what is up with the images of young men these days? Everybody has to be tough. This macho hate-stare thing has got to go. Like it's against the law to be friendly. As if that's anti-man. This is why so many kids carry weapons. If a man is supposed to be hard, as tough as a brick, with the emotional feelings of a toaster, then carrying a gun makes sense. It makes you an instant man, without having to go through all the mental gymnastics of things that make an adult's head hurt, like telling the difference between right and wrong. So put some HAPPY people on the wall. Lot's of them. "Gee, I don't know why my child has such a negative view of life." Well, if manhood has been defined by negative images, what do you expect? And ladies, you can help here, you know, by not encouraging the modern hate man. If you are attracted by the fact that your boyfriend can't hold a job and is only seconds away from becoming violently unhinged, you need to give Oprah or Phil a call and talk this thing out. And stop dancing to songs that call you disgraceful things. I mean, if the band was joyfully playing "You're a four eyed white trash idiot" I don't think you'd find me on the dance floor doing the Glide.

Which leads me to audio imaging. What you hear is almost as important as what you see and all of the same rules apply. Keep what a child hears positive in nature. A young teacher at a faculty meeting once said, "You know, it's not Aretha Franklin any more. It's kill, kill, murder, murder." What an eloquent observation. Listen to some Motown from the sixties. The Supreme's "Stop In The Name Of Love" would now be "Stop, You B…. Before I Snap Your Collarbone".

Control, for as long as you can, what your child hears. The ears are a direct conduit to the brain, which is what we are trying to build up. If your four year old is exposed to constant cursing don't be shocked when "Grandpa" becomes " that blankety blank old blank."

When I say control what a child hears, I am not just talking about hovering over the CD player. What, as a PARENT, you say to your child carries more weight than what anybody on the planet can say. So, for heaven's sake, don't EVER call your child stupid or any other adjective that implies stupid. I don't care what kind of stupid thing that child has done. You can find him in the middle of your beloved flower garden munching on your Zinnias while he is burying your only car key and you still can't impugn his brain capacity, because he will internalize it. It will become his world view. If you call your child a mean, disrespectful, lazy imbecile, be prepared for the phone call from school saying that your little Shirley flunked her test, slept through class, cursed the teacher when she woke her, and beat up Shonterrica because she was looking at her the wrong way. You shake your head sadly. "I just don't know what got into her." What do you mean you don't know what got into her? YOU got into her.

So you've got to find a positive way of addressing a child when they mess up. I suggest practice BEFORE a child messes up, because it's hard to do when you are furious and yelling. I'm going to talk about discipline, per se, in a minute, but this is it's foundation: *It's not the child you are mad at, but the ridiculous BEHAVIOR that he is exhibiting. This is so important that it is not just rule number one, but actually rule one through twenty.* If the parent internalizes this, then positive discipline becomes much easier. Basically, you're not mad at your youngster, but at the fact that he has somehow now learned how to spell misdemeanor. If a child feels that you love them and you have their best interest at heart, they will accept any reasonable discipline you mete out. If a child feels that you hate them, then it becomes a battle of whether or not you have the ability to make them obey. A child is going to respond to where they think that discipline is coming from. Always lead with a positive, self-image building statement, THEN put the hammer down.

An example: I used to work at a last chance type of facility that kids were sent to for zero tolerance offenses, usually fighting or drugs. Sometimes fighting over the drugs while on the drugs. They're basically good kids with a very limited and violent set of tools to deal with life. Occasionally I'd get a call in my office from a teacher telling me that a student was out of control in their class. Since my job title was Mr. Control, I would go to the room and remove the student so the teacher could perform his job title. Let's say I'm dealing with Franco, who weighs 220 lbs. and is sixteen years old. The very first thing that comes out of my mouth when I enter the room is "Now, Franco, you know I love you. Love you all day long. And I have all the faith in the world that you are going to become the highly paid and highly qualified auto mechanic that you are striving to become because you are a genius with cars, but writing profanity on Sherita's backside with her own eye liner is unacceptable. Come with me, please." They would always come with no further trouble. Why? I did not attack them, so there was nothing to defend. I told the child one, I love them, two, that everything I do is to ensure a brighter future, that I believe they HAVE a brighter future, and finally, that I will punish, if need be, to ensure that bright future. And I have set the stage, in a positive way, for any escalation of force that is needed. *Children will accept any and all discipline if it comes from a positive place.*

How is Franco's self image after all this? Absolutely intact. During this uproar he has been loved and called competent to the point of genius. That's exactly what I want, because if he believes that about himself he will react accordingly during the punishment phase. What I'll get is, "I'm sorry. I know I can do better. I promise." And he will, in fact, do so.

Gentlemen, does a grown man saying "I love you" to a male teenager seem a little strange to you? Sure it does. And that's too bad. It seems strange because, first of all, you think love means sex, which it doesn't because they are two completely different things. And second of all, many males don't have fathers so they have never heard it in their entire life.

You know the reaction I would get when I walk into a room and say "You know I love you but"…..? At first, of course, laughter and disbelief. After awhile, however, when I'd enter the room to deal with a situation, I'd be greeted with a chorus of "We love you Mr. Johnson." I'd follow with, " Ah, yes, I'm full of love today. It's a beautiful day. Now Johnny, untie Mr. Jefferson, please. And give me the sword before you hurt somebody."

Males of all ages are literally dying to hear "I love you" coming from a father figure. They are beating and stabbing and shooting and hating each other because no man in their life has taken the time to show them that being a man is love, not hardness, coldness, toughness, meanness, hate. Gentlemen, I am going to repeat this one more time. DO NOT RUN OUT ON YOUR CHILDREN. YOU ARE MORE IMPORTANT THAN YOU THINK.

To review: positive self image is, one, lead with I love you but...., you are a genius but....or whatever positive phrase you want. Two, tie to destiny self-image. "You're going to be a great dress designer someday, but........", then the discipline that seems appropriate.

One last word on building a positive self-image in your child. Empty praise will not get you there. "Oh, Brandon, that was great. You are so smart. Daddy is so proud of you." DON'T say all of this when all the child has done is sneezed all over himself. You can say I love you all day long, but save the praise for when they've actually done something. Praise the accomplishment. "Brandon, you mowed the entire lawn and left the rose bushes intact this time. Great job." Or, "Barbara, you've memorized all of your times tables. That's very smart, girl. Now we can apply it to your trigonometry homework."

By praising accomplishments, or good efforts towards a goal, the child's positive self-image that she is building will stand the child in good stead later on in life when it gets tough because it was based on reality. The child is developing faith in her own mental and physical abilities to reach a goal. This is hugely important. If child "A" has a goal of earning a good income and faith in his own abilities to do so, he may spend his time steering towards his goal through studies and hard work. If child "B" has the same goal, but no faith in his abilities to achieve it, he will spend his time stalking child "A".

Ability based praise will build an adult who is confident and competent. Empty praise, just to make the child feel good, will build a swelled head and a sense of entitlement much like a spoiled rotten prince who demands to take a pony from another child simply because he is the king's son. Or the CEO who thinks he deserves a 200 million dollar severance package even though the company is going into the dump.

Faith in ability will get a child through hard as well as good times. Faith in entitlement only works if everything is flowing your way, like being lucky enough to be born to the king instead of the hot, sweaty blacksmith down the street, who actually works for a living.

How can you tell what kind of child you've got? Ask them what they want to do in life. If they reply lay on the couch all day, and mean it, you have a large, expensive entitlement problem on your hands.

And don't think for one second that you're fooling the kid with your empty praise. When I was in junior high school I could be told all day long by well meaning adults about how great a dancer I was, but I knew in reality I was going to make a big, fat fool out of myself the very second I hit the dance floor. I knew my ability level, as all children do, so I would spend dance night terrified and sick. "Oh, Martha, what an exquisite piece of art. It's beautiful. And at your age." "Mom, it's a purple line. My hand slipped. And I just turned twenty-six." So, please stick with ability, effort, and success based praise.

I'm going to touch on routines for a moment. So far we've laid an excellent foundation for raising a success oriented child. It will help greatly if you stick to certain routines each day, such as bed time, meal time, reading time, and play time with you. At first glance children seem to like chaos. A close reading of "Lord of the Flies" shows that kids may gravitate to chaos, but not necessarily like it. Children's brains are constantly trying to create order in the middle of disorder. Give a group of children some toys and tell them to play, with no other instructions than to just have fun. What are the kids going to do? Spend two hours arguing over the rules. Guaranteed. If you have routines that are consistent, it frees the child's mind up for other things besides trying to create order, such as thinking, learning and creating. If you don't have any consistency in the house the child's mind will be constantly testing and probing where some boundaries are and the thinking and learning thing will take a back seat. Case in point. Larry is going home from school, as he always does at four o'clock. He runs to the house to be greeted by mom, as always. Except this time mom is not there. No note. Just not there. It's an empty house. Now, what is Larry going to do? Is he going to meticulously lay out all of his homework, books, pencils and get to work so that he is done by dinner? Or is he going to rip his hair out as he runs frantically from room to room searching for his mother, because she may have run off with a motorcycle gang and is right now driving wildly through the mountains of North Carolina, like she's been threatening to do for the last ten years.

There is not a child on this planet that would sit down and do his homework under those circumstances. What if it happens a lot? What if mom and dad are missing a lot and the child doesn't know where they are? What do you think that child is thinking about at school? Geometry? What if some days there is food and other days not? What if sometimes he goes to bed at nine o'clock and other times at one o'clock in the morning? What if sometimes dad is sweet and playful and other times violent and moody?

Consistency is very important for a child's learning ability and routines are a way for that consistency to be formalized in your house. Consistency is the cornerstone for learning. All science and math are based on it. How could the adult mind function if gravity was just an occasional thing? Sometimes hot air rises and sometimes it falls? Have a carpool bet each morning on which direction the sun will rise from?

The human brain is an ordering, organizing machine. If there was no sense to the universe, if everything was random, the brain would go mad spending all it's time trying to create some semblance of order. If there is no order in your house, which is the child's universe, their brain will spend most of it's energy trying to figure out WHAT in the heck is going on.

The only thing your child is going to learn is the fine art of arguing. And not the logic based type of arguing that might do her some good when she is a lawyer. No, no. We're talking chaos based arguing here. "Why do I have to go to bed now? You let me watch the "Late, Late Show" last night. Why do I have to read today? I got to watch TV all last year. You didn't say anything then. What do you mean I can't drink beer today? You let me last Tuesday. So, what, Tuesday is beer day or something? Let me know when it's crack day. That's the one I don't want to miss."

Consistency is all the more important in your home, because the school that your child is going to attend could be Anarchy High, named after the children who didn't get any structure at their home. And if they don't get structure at home or at school, they'll probably end up at Structure University, which is prison. The voluntary one is the military.

One routine I'd like to emphasize is bedtime. Plenty of sleep is important for children. Not only is this when the body repairs itself, but the brain processes the day's information also. Memory and information retrieval paths are being worked on as well as all of the emotional drama of the day. If your child is punching the pillow in his sleep while yelling, "I hate algebra but mostly I hate you, Mrs. Davis", don't worry. It's perfectly normal. It's just a reminder to call the school early the next morning.

This memory consolidation thing is kind of important. It helps not just in real life, but in school too. "Mrs. Klein, your son can't remember half of his spelling words or any of his times tables. Does he get enough sleep at night?" "Well, let me see. He did get in a couple of hours last Thursday. We've been celebrating Octoberfest recently." "Mrs. Klein, it's April 5th. Why don't we give it a rest for a little bit?"

I have a word of advice. If you don't want your child to learn anything, don't send him to school in the first place. Just stay up all night playing cards in the attic, where the authorities can't find you. Even if the authorities do find your child you won't get into any trouble. He won't be able to remember his OR your name. You're in the clear.

PLEASE establish a good bedtime. The bedtime routine is great, because a lot of other routines can be built around it. Reading a book out loud, recapping the day, prayer and giving thanks, if that is what your religion dictates. I realize that some religions dictate blowing up the bed, but in most households reading, conversation and prayers seem to suffice.

We are getting near to the end of our time here. Let's see what we've got. We've got a healthy child with a strong emotional and intellectual foundation for success in life, because you've followed the plan that you've set forth for her upbringing. A good, solid, adult plan. The problem is, the child hates the adult plan because it clashes with the child's plan, which is to anything he or she wants, whenever they want to do it. The child doesn't want the adult plan because he's obviously not intent on living long enough to actually be an adult. It is up to you to make sure that they live until their 18th birthday. If they die an unnatural death before 18, it's on you. After 18, it's their bad.

How in the world are you going to execute your well thought out success plan when every facet of our society, every where you turn, is trying to tell your child to do the exact opposite? And he, of course, agrees with them.

Because you are the child's PARENTS. Not friend, neighbor, cousin, acquaintance, roommate or homey. The ROLE of parent is unique. It means, by the laws of nature, that you are IN CHARGE. Now, like all businesses, if you don't want to be the boss, then don't apply for the job, because you will find a horde of employees who are depending on you for their livelihood staring anxiously at you, waiting to see what to do next. If shrugging your shoulders or hiding in the alley so they don't see you cry are the two best options that you can come up with, it is a sign that you are not boss material.

But if you have come to the stage of life where you feel the competence to actually be the boss, be the parent, then do so, because children do not raise themselves. Raise is a verb, which means that a parent has to actually do something, which is why you carry your success parenting plan in your back pocket, where it is handy.

This "in charge" deal needs to be established, however. The child isn't born knowing who's in charge. In fact, he is born thinking that he is in charge. Of everything. Is, in fact, the center of the entire universe. And a bright kid with an interest in physics will tell you that he is the center of all the parallel universes also.

Besides safety, the single most important thing that a parent can do is establish the RIGHT OF LEGITIMATE AUTHORITY in the child's mind. Early. The first thing you do is take the infant over to a celestial map and point out that, not only is he not the center of the universe, but not even the center of his own little solar system. This little tidbit of information will not be welcomed, as Galileo and a host of jailed and beaten mathematicians were to find out in earlier times. You, as a parent, have a distinct advantage over Galileo, however. You are bigger than your adversary. Use the advantage now, because it won't always be that way. You are also smarter. For now. Don't let the moment slip away.

What is legitimate authority? The fact that, as a

child, and later as an adult, we mutually agree as a society that there are times that we have to do as we are told, even if we don't like it. And that there are certain roles that we play as adults that give us the right to tell others what to do. And if we abide by these roles, we can enjoy the fruits of what is called civilization, as opposed to life in a mosh pit.

Decree number one is that a child MUST listen to his parents. Period. Debate is over. Debate never even began. If you can't enforce decree number one, then burn all of your other decrees because your empire will crumble to dust as the Vandals and Huns have a picnic in downtown Rome.

This is not being mean. It's not being unfair. This is simply the way it works. And it's for the child's own good because, unbeknownst to him, his very survival depends on this parent-child relationship. And, really, there is no other way that it can work. Even a child knows that. Even a child who has lost her mind knows that. I was in a student-parent meeting once and the fourteen year old student started cursing at her mother. I pulled her aside, literally, and asked her if she would allow her own child to talk to her like that. She looked at me like I was crazy. "No child of mine is going to curse me. They are going to RESPECT me."

R..E..S..P..E..C..T. Respect is how we acknowledge legitimate authority. It is the glue that holds society together. It is a courteous nod to the ROLE: parent, teacher, police officer, firefighter, etc. When the child was cursing her mother she wasn't just showing her contempt for Sally, the person, but for the role of mother itself. And if the ROLE of mother is disrespected, as in "I don't have to listen to my mother", which translates into "I don't have to listen to anybody on this planet", which really means "can somebody whom I haven't offended yet please send me bail money?"

So, how does a child, who clearly knows better, end up cursing out her mother? Because she can. It has never been established IN HER MIND that what she is doing is unacceptable. One of the casualties of never learning respect is having no self-respect. The question now is, how do you get respect for legitimate authority into a child's mind? You start from infancy. You make it a natural rule of law. There is gravity, electro-magnetic forces, laws of inertia and parents are in charge of the family and are to be respected. The child will accept all this as normal, which frees his mind up to go about the business of being a child. If this parent-child role isn't established then your child thinks that he is a co-equal adult. Co-equal if you're lucky. You will have a tiny, immature but forceful adult to argue with about anything. You don't EVER want your child to think that they are your equal, unless your idea of a good conversation is begging and pleading. And I mean coming from you. You might as well invite a midget version of Ghengis Khan to move in with you. Tyrant comes from the Latin word meaning toddler.

And you better establish this child-parent relationship early. You don't want to wait until they're sixteen and interrupt them while they're cleaning their AK-47 to have a talk about who's boss in the house. Besides, if you don't establish who's boss early, you can't ever use the parent's short but brilliantly effective motivational tool, which is, "Because I said so." The only way that works is if the word "I", meaning parent, actually stands for something. If the child views you as Timmy The Big Turnip, then "Because I said so" doesn't carry much weight. There is nothing wrong with discussing or even negotiating a decision with your child. But negotiating after the decision has been made is called surrender. An ill-tempered buck private is now running your household because the general abdicated his authority.

When giving a command, you don't want a child thinking that now it's time for them to weigh their options. "Let's see, should I run blindly out into the street risking instant death or paralysis OR should I go to mommy who is, as I ponder, yelling at me to get back from the curb. What to do, what to do?" How about DO AS YOU'RE TOLD? This is not congress, where you get to debate endlessly and then do nothing. This is real life here. The small child debating society holds it's meetings in hospitals, because that's where most of its members reside. The ones in the cemetery didn't make the debate team...... What's that? I'm ruining your Saturday? Well, yes, I guess the death of a child will do that. Probably put a damper on Sunday through Friday, also. That's precisely why we are spending this wonderful quality time together today. If there is no parent role to say no and have it obeyed, bad junk happens. Cemetery, hospital, courthouse, prison: these are the playgrounds for children who feel they don't have to listen to anybody, and not one of those places has the word university attached to it..........You look upset, sweetheart. Sex is a strange business. It has a lot of baggage that goes with it: emotionally, physically, spiritually. It has all of these side avenues that you don't even think about when you're fifteen. As a parent, you have to think about unpleasant things, though. You don't have the luxury of ignoring the consequences, of pretending, which is child-think. What, exactly, do you suppose a small child is going to do when your back is turned for even one second? The very SECOND you're not looking that child is going to go explore his world, which translates into, "Martha, you better run get your boy because it looks like he's trying to kill himself." You don't know what they're going to do, except that it involves bodily harm. Now, you can have a child when you're fifteen if you want to, but when your hair turns shock white when you're seventeen, I don't want to hear about it...... I see. You thought that parents bossing you around was just because they want to micro-manage your life, as if they didn't have enough to do. I am sure it seems that way sometimes. It's all about their intense fear of losing someone as precious as you. Little Luellen: "I hope she doesn't fall and hurt herself." Big Luellen out on a date: "I hope she gets home on time and doesn't die in a flaming car wreck." It'll be that way, no matter what your age. If you are old and in a walker and your mother is still alive, it'll be like the old days. She'll be worried about you falling and hurting yourself again. It is in the nature of the relationship. What you don't want is, "Where's Luellen?" "I don't know, who cares?"

To recap: you have GOT to establish parental authority in your house for the safety and welfare of the child. O.K., Mr. Authority, all dressed up in your fancy authority uniform, feeling powerful, lord of the house and lawn, Mr. Because I Said So: you have just asked your child to do something and they look up at you with that adoring, cute little face and respond with, "NO!" Don't look shocked. The child still loves you. It's just what we in the education field call a teachable moment. If your child has never said a defiant "NO" to you it's because you've never asked them to do anything besides eat ice cream and watch television. Now, there are many ways for a general to deal with open rebellion. There are whole books written on the subject. Pick one off the shelf and use it, because if the rebellion succeeds the coup de tat is over and you are now looking at a life of perpetual k-p duty and walking the perimeter. I am going to tell you a true story. I was outside in my yard, which I earned by working for a living. I asked my son to pick up some sticks and put them in the wheelbarrow so that I could mow the lawn safely. He's a little surly because he'd rather be inside watching TV, so I decided to make a game out of it, which I often try to do with chores. I started throwing sticks in from different parts of the yard. I began to notice that I was the only one working on my jump shot, however, so I again asked him to help. He said that he didn't feel like it because his back hurt. Two things ran through my mind at the same time. One, was the fact that his back didn't seem to hurt much when he was doing flips in the air conditioned living room and two, was that he didn't seem overly concerned about the fact that I had a long week and maybe my back was bothering me, too. I asked him ever so politely, but a little more firmly, to help me in the yard. This time he said a little more firmly, "I don't feel like it." The yard was no longer my focal point. "Son, this work needs to be done and I need your help." "Why do I have to bend over and pick up sticks. They're not really bothering anything." "Because I'm your father and I said so. Start over there and put them in the cart, NOW." I've gone from asking to telling. That's when it came rolling out. "NO!" It probably surprised him as much as me. He had never flat out said "NO" before. So there it was, for all the world to see. I measured my words carefully. "Son, you are a great kid and I love you, but you are going to pick up these sticks. If I have to spank you to do so, so be it. It's your choice. Are you going to fill that wheelbarrow, or not?" He was a good kid and like all kids had been punished before, by time-outs, no TV or loss of privileges, but he had never been spanked before because he had never put himself in the position to be spanked, which, to me, is showing open defiance. We eyeballed each other a little more but evidently the mere threat of a spanking didn't do it. He had made up his mind. "NO!" The spanking itself lasted two seconds at most and wasn't particularly painful, but the effect was electric. I had a yard to be proud of and, after the weeping and sobbing was over, one in which I could enjoy time with my family. And my family was intact again. Each person, parent and child, was back firmly in their proper role. You know what my son said later on that day? ......No, he didn't curse me. He said, "I'm sorry dad." This implied several things, including the knowledge that he was wrong and didn't blame me for correcting the situation. I told him that I loved him and was sorry that I had to do what I had to do. We laughed at the basic stupidity of the whole incident and went on about our day.

I had an enlightening moment at an Academy once. We had a girl, who I will call Suzie, go ballistic, trying to kick out the windows and doors of the office and assault everybody in an attempt to run away. While the police were taking the young lady away in handcuffs and putting her into the back seat of the police car, an adult volunteer at the school looked at me and said, "you know, there's something terribly wrong here. Society is willing to put this girl in jail, but think it's wrong to spank her to prevent it." No truer words have ever been spoken. I am not advocating spanking, per se, but there must be a fair but severe punishment designed for open rebellion. Saving the family unit is that important. This girl had always run her household and as she got older it got less and less funny. Unless something is done she will end up trying to rule over a bunch of girls just like her. Being boss in a prison is not quite as easy as whipping up on a ninety pound aunt or throwing grandma down a flight of stairs. Every member of a family should have to sign a contract stipulating that, no matter what they do, it will not involve destroying the family unit because, in reality, that's all that most of us have that stands between a decent standard of living and living in a tin lean-to and eating on the soup line. Nobody is allowed to step out of their assigned role. The child cannot be the adult, as we've seen, and the adult cannot be the child, which happens a lot also. "Dad, where are you going?" "To the strip club." "But Dad, it's a school night. How about a little help here?"

A lot of this mess is not of Suzie's own making.

Her family was so dysfunctional that she never learned what a child's place is in the family, or really what a family is besides a collection of relatives in a house. Being a head of a family, with all it's complexities, is like driving a speeding train. In this particular family, they let tiny Casey Jones climb into the cab and be the engineer. We all know how that turned out. The worst part about tiny Casey Jones is that she is like Jason: she never dies. Just walks away from the train wreck and jumps aboard another train. If the family is destroyed, what next? Casey sees the train marked "school" and scrambles on board that one. Not in the rear, of course. She heads straight for the engineer's seat.

    As a teacher, you can tell the students a mile away who run their own homes. When they enter school they full well expect to run the classroom, and don't mind who knows it. And if you ask them to do something that they don't feel like doing, they'll turn all lawyer on you. "I know my rights." Let me give you the reasoned response of Thomas Jefferson, author of the Declaration of Independence and one of the founders of the concept of the public school system. And I quote: "What are you talking about? You have no rights. Have you lost your mind? Have you been drinking before school again? Sit down and do your work. Adults have rights. Eighteen years old and up. You are an adult in training, which is called a child. Don't ever talk back to me again or I'll put my boot upside your head just like I did to the British." "I know my rights." Don't make me laugh. And if you don't establish the parent-child relationship early, that's all any adult is ever going to hear from your kid:

"I know my rights."

"Why do the Asians do so well in school?" I heard a mother pondering this while she was waiting for her child to come out of the principal's office. " I don't understand how, out of a student body of 1,500 people, only two of whom are Asian, both of them were tied for class valedictorian." Well, Kim Wong didn't spend one second of her time trying to figure out who the teacher was in the class, her or the older person. She put all her energies into her studies. When she boarded the train, she didn't run to the cab to hijack it. She got into the passenger car with her laptop. By the time Casey Jones had her wreck, Kim was putting the finishing touches on a new aerodynamic design so that the train would run more efficiently.

The whole point here is that discipline is good for the child as well as for the family and society. Essential for the child because it takes a lot of the foolishness out of the ball game so that the child can focus their energies on positive things. As a teacher, the number two phrase that you are likely to hear after making a request of a student, right after "I know my rights" is "You're not my daddy." What a breath taking statement this is. And what a revealing one. There is no further proof needed of the damage done to a child when there is no father present in their life than the bitter shouting of, "You're not my daddy!" when asked to do something by an authority figure. For a teacher it is an invaluable statement because it tells volumes about the child. Ninety-nine out of a hundred times it tells me that the child has no father. And they aren't too happy about it. And they're so hacked off about being abandoned that they aren't going to let you or any other do-gooder adult fill the role because, as has been forcefully and eloquently stated, "You're not my daddy." It's when they erupt with "You're not my daddy" or it's cousin "You can't make me", that the extent of the damage becomes clear. Children usually go through the "you can't make me" stage around two years old. The official medical term for this stage is the terrible twos. Another something for you would-be parents to look forward to. The stage ends when they are actually MADE to do something, which usually involves a lot of crying, kicking and screaming. Once the child realizes he is not the CEO of the company, but a stockroom clerk instead, life returns to normal. If there is no authority figure in the house it is virtually impossible for the child to ever have a normal life. You have got a two year old stuck in a sixteen year old body. Just a heads up here. I have no idea how the dating thing works anymore, but I have a feeling that most teenagers of the opposite sex are not turned on by infants. Let me tell you two real life stories.

    I had a parent-teacher conference once with a teenaged boy being raised by his grandmother. She said to me, "Mr. Johnson, I think you're being too hard on Kevin. You should do what I do when he gets really angry. I lock myself in the bathroom and after a couple of hours he calms down." The principal explained to her that our classrooms weren't equipped with bathrooms to hide in, so that wasn't an option. She was very understanding. Now, bless her heart, she was doing the best that she could. But her best wasn't helping her grandson any. Later in the year I ended up taking a gun and bullets from the young man. I still have the bullets in my den. That poor woman should never have been in this position. Where was the rest of the family unit?

I had another young man, around sixteen years old, who would start every class with a defiant "you can't make me read." Think about that one for a moment. What a profound window into his world view. That's his entire life. "You can't make me eat." Yeah, O.K. You've got a point. Unfortunately, this sets young adults up for the "yes, we can make you" hotel, which is jail. And the juvenile justice system in the United States is so ineffective, that it isn't until the clang of a prison cell reverberates in their ears that their "You can't make me" world actually crumbles. What a waste of a life. This is why proper parenting is so important and why I am spending my Saturday here doing my best to drive you crazy.

Now, I myself am crazier than most teachers and took the "you can't make me read" as a personal challenge. I, in fact MADE him read. It was a daily adventure into the world of professional wrestling. Ten years later he returned to say hello. He was dressed in his full military uniform. He said that because he could read he got to ride in the tank instead of being relegated to menial duties, such as washing the tank. This is the entire reasoning for good parenting. I have said this before but it's worth repeating. EVERY child has a success destiny. It is up to the parent to instill the skills and set the foundation for that success. Which brings me to the phrase "tough love."

Since your generation is eaten up with the

desire for tattoos and is rushing headlong to have babies to raise, I suggest that you have "tough love" tattooed someplace real prominent on your body so that you won't forget it. Like across your forehead. I think branding would actually be better, because you could feel it as well as see it.

Tough love means that you will do whatever it takes to make your child a success. The secret is the word tough. It really applies to YOU, not your child. You better be tough. If crying, begging or whining pushes your buttons, don't become a parent. Or school teacher for that matter. Because you will cave in like a cardboard house in a thunderstorm. When you cave in, you are training that child to be a whining, complaining, dysfunctional, miserable adult. And boy, aren't they fun to be around? You'll see as you get older. They're called co-workers.

I have a concrete suggestion. Once a decision is made, stick with it and don't let the child whine or beg. Cut the conversation off immediately, only to return when a normal tone of voice returns. This is one of those "don't do this" real life stories. "Mom, may I have an ice cream bar?" "No, honey, it's too close to dinner." "But, mom, I'm hungry and dinner is almost an hour away." "No, ice cream is not to be eaten until after dinner." "I'll eat all my dinner, I promise." "Listen, honey, I've got work to do. Please go and watch television." "But I'm hungry mom. Please let me have an ice cream bar. I'll be quiet and I promise I'll eat my dinner." "Oh, O.K., go ahead. But don't disturb me until dinner." "Yes, mom", as she skips merrily off to get her hard-earned ice cream bar.

What you just witnessed was the building of a Frankenstein Monster, without all the messy body parts. Like it or not, every adult, and especially every parent is a ROLE MODEL. The monkey see, monkey do principal in living color, everyday. What did this well meaning and hard working mother just teach her child? .... You got it. That she doesn't mean what she says. That her mind can be changed, which guarantees what kind of response from the child?........That's right. An argument. Every time. How's that child going to respond in school when the teacher asks her to do something? "Connie, your assignment tonight is page 56, #1-30. What's that? No, #1-15 will not suffice. Yes, I'm sure that #1-15 is probably enough to show competency but I asked for #1-30 for a reason. There are other competencies in the latter 15 that I want to check. No, doing #10-20 is not an option either." And so it goes.

There was an experiment done with chickens that illustrates this point so clearly that I still marvel at it. The scientists wanted to see what the optimum reward system is to keep a chicken begging for food the longest. All the chickens had a button to peck to receive a food pellet. One set of chickens got rewarded with every peck, one set every two pecks, one set every three pecks, etc., all the way to one pellet for every ten pecks. They were trained for a long time to respond to this exact reward system. Then the scientist stopped giving any food pellets. Now the experiment starts. Which chicken do you think pecked the longest in its now futile search for food? Think about it for a minute..........Yes? .... How about you young man?...............Interesting. Young lady?............... Very interesting. You're on the right track. What we actually had was this: The chicken that was used to a consistent reward system, one peck, one pellet, quit wasting his time first. He knew that nothing was coming, so he quit trying. The one with the next most consistent reward system, two pecks for one pellet, soon after stopped trying. The lesson to be learned, as parents, is that the chicken who got rewarded very inconsistently, the ratio being seven pecks for every one pellet, kept pecking the button almost forever after the food stopped. Is probably still pecking now, as we speak. "Mommy, can I have some ice cream?" "No. No. No. No. No. No. Oh, all right, just make sure it doesn't spoil your dinner." BINGO. That child has just sprouted feathers. She is chicken number seven. She will never accept what she is told without an argument. She is probably still arguing about the pay raise that she didn't get ten years ago. So, to save your child's adulthood, wear that tough love brand on your forehead proudly and mean it. Always be consistent with your children.

To help with the consistency deal, there are a few rules that you and your spouse need to discuss and agree on before you ever ask your child to do one, single, thing.

Don't ever say or promise the child anything before OK'ing it with your spouse first. Have these discussions away from the child. If you say something like, "you know, it seems like a good day to go to the movies" and the child can hear you, you are in fact going to the movies that day, good day or not. Don't make suggestions of any kind within earshot of a child, because then they are no longer suggestions. In that child's mind they are a reality. You have now put yourself in a terrible position. You either end up doing something that, in retrospect, wasn't a great idea, like losing your job because you told junior that you would take him to a ball game during the day. Or you have to change your mind, in which case you have set yourself up for a wrestling match with your child, which could easily morph into the tag-team match from Hades if your darling spouse is also angry at whatever stupid thing came out of your mouth. Adults are so used to speaking to other adults and weighing whether that person is a liar or just a politician that we have a tendency to forget that most children, for a period of time, actually believe that what an adult says is the truth. I'm still stewing over the fact that, when I was ten years old, I was promised one dollar per plug of Zoisia Grass that I helped my father and a neighbor put in. It never occurred to me that the neighbor was "just joking", as my father put it the next day. I thought that maybe I was born defective, not having a sense of humor and all, because I didn't see what was funny about getting gypped out of two hundred dollars. As a matter of fact, I still don't. I STILL want my money, and my trust in adults, back. Right now I'd settle for the money.

    On a similar note, it is always best to think before you speak, especially if you are going to make a request or demand of your child. DON'T say things you don't mean, because you have got to go through with what has just escaped from your mouth; otherwise you have just gone from consistent parent to poultry farmer, wondering why your chickens won't listen to you. "Go to your room and finish all of your homework. I don't care that it's five hours worth.

You are not having dinner until you have finished. And if it's not done by morning, no breakfast, either." Now, Mr. Big Man, you have just stuffed yourself into a box in which you can't possibly fit. You have made two huge mistakes. You have said words that you will have to eat later, which may be just as well, because it's probably the only dinner that you are going to get anyway. The other mistake is not noticing that your wife is behind you cutting vegetables with a sharp knife while you are making a fool out of yourself screaming at her only child.

There is actually a third mistake here and that is punishing in anger. Anger is the beast that drives bad parenting and bad teaching. Everybody gets angry but nobody thinks clearly when upset. The best antidote for parenting by anger is to have a plan for what to do when a child needs correction. The plan is best developed before he needs correction. You know that your child is going to mess up, so don't be shocked by it. Just be ready for it, that's all. I read a quote by Plato or Socrates years ago, which for me puts everything in perspective. I guess that some ancient teenage hoodlum had done something to infuriate the great one, because he went on a rant about how disrespectful, violent, disobedient, lazy and generally worthless teenagers were. He went on to mention that they were not only a threat to society, but threatened the very existence of civilization itself. I thought to myself, how refreshing. It says to me that children have always been children and will always be children, for good or for bad. So if you are shocked by misbehaviors, don't be a parent, teacher, or any other profession dealing with children because misbehaving is what psychiatrists call normal. It is your response to it that separates good parent from bad, good teacher from bad, good police officer from bad.

Sit down with your spouse and concoct a misbehavior correction plan. Don't wait until you get a call from the police department to come pick your son up to formulate your plan. That plan will probably have elements in it that are frowned upon by most judicial systems, such as pain and death. So come up with a plan. When Cheryl acts out in public, what will we do? Spanking is a very limited option, should be used only for open defiance, should be given as a choice that the child is going to make, and used very infrequently. In public it is not an option at all, unless you enjoy explaining to a SWAT team why you are having to discipline your child. A good option is removal. Instant and swift. The secret to any effective discipline is instant and swift. That's the power of a proper spanking, as opposed to a beating. It is not the pain that is the prime motivating tool. So, if your child throws a fit in a store over some thing that he feels that he is entitled to and you are refusing to buy because, unlike the adults he sees on TV, you are not a millionaire, simply declare the shopping excursion over and march him promptly out of the store, kicking and screaming. I prefer throwing him over my shoulder for dramatic effect, but that is just a style preference. Either way, the child is stunned by the forcefulness of your actions and usually taken aback by the rounds of applause that will spontaneously burst forth from other adults in the store, who are sick of hearing him whine also and relieved that at least SOMEBODY out there is taking the time to raise his child properly. Explain to the child that the ticket to public places is proper behavior, and he will have the PRIVILEGE of going to public places when, and only when, he can act accordingly. The learning curve is even more electric if you pick your places of removal cunningly. Removal from a birthday party at Chuck E. Cheese is a mind blower. The child will learn more in five minutes than thirty hours of father-son lectures. The trick is to PLAN to do this, or anything similar. If your child has been misbehaving lately, take him to someplace that he would like to go, but one in which you have no real interest in. When he is removed, it has cost you nothing and him everything.

Removal of PRIVILEGES is another good tool. What is a privilege? Anything except food, water, air and shelter. Take the TV, toys, electronic equipment of any kind. Whatever. I have a form at school that I hand to parents of teenagers. All a parent has to do is sign it and the form goes straight to the highway patrol department. The child will NEVER get a driver's license until the parent signs a release form. Now, THAT is an attention getter........... Proper etiquette states that it is never polite to boo the professor. Evidently we are forgetting why it is that we are disciplining a child. Parenting is WORK, with a capitol "W", and all of this work is to ensure that a child becomes a successful adult, whether they particularly like it or not. The hardest part about parenting, especially for very young parents, is that everything you do needs to fit into a long term, goal oriented plan. If you are almost a child your own self, that is a very hard mental leap to make, because the younger you are, the more short term goal oriented you are. A perfect example is a budget. Young lady, what does your budget look like?......... Of course you don't have one. You should have one, but you don't. You're only fourteen. I am fifty four. I have one. You're thinking changes as you get older.

Back to practical success oriented discipline tips. It is very important that the adults in the family communicate with each other and stay on the same page. That includes grandma. Children will look for the weakest link in the fence to try to escape parental authority. Don't let a child play one adult against the other. They will play them better than they do their Gameboy. If your child comes running to you from the direction of another adult asking for something, what you don't say is "yes." They are running from that adult because they just said "no" and are coming to you because you look like a sucker. What you ask is, "what did mommy say?" And stick with it. The parents may want to have a private discussion later about what mommy said, but mom and dad and uncle and grandma need to back each other up in front of that child. Consistency. Clear vision. Clear expectations. Family unity. Family purpose.

We are at an interesting point in history. A well functioning family is needed more than ever now, and yet they seem to be harder and harder to find. There are a couple of things going on in the background that are contributing to this. One is a divorce rate so high that most kids have never seen how a family is supposed to work. In the famous marital advice given to a newlywed by Ed Norton from the Honeymooners, "If you don't want to fight, what are you getting married for?" Another trend is economic. This idea of the "working poor" is ridiculous. Pay scales so low that people have to work five jobs to stay afloat, while nobody is left at home to give any kind of guidance to their children. A long time ago it was called slavery but that term has a slightly negative connotation these days, so corporations call it "working poor" instead. It used to be that if you had a latchkey kid you would be put in the system for child abandonment. Now it's O.K. to leave your children alone, raised by violent and disrespectful and destructive images coming off of the surrogate parent, the TV screen, because profits have become more important than our own children. So, do what you can to create your own, real, loving family unit, because that is the best defense you and your child will have against an increasingly cold world.

"Whew. Let the professor sit for a second after that rant. Boy, I feel better now. Sometimes it feels good to get stuff off your chest. Whew, again. Why don't we take a ten minute bathroom break and then we'll wrap this up so that you can spend the rest of your Saturday in deep meditative contemplation. Or wild abandonment. Whatever...............

Alright, let's wrap this bad boy up. I appreciate your attentiveness today. It is my hope that somewhere in the midst of all this boring mishmash that you have learned something of value today that you can carry home with you. Now that you have raised your child well and prepared him as best you can to be a success in school, what do you do once he is actually in school? My best advice is two-fold. First, I would get to know the teachers personally, as human beings. Invite them over for dinner. Teachers are poor. They love free dinners. Once a bond is established, then you've got a group of human beings doing their best for your child, which is all that one can ask. It also rephrases the "what are you doing to my child?" to "what did my child do to you and how far should I throw him?", which is music to a teacher's ears. Now you've got a REAL bond established. Which brings me to my second word of advice. Let them do their job.

I have a friend named Nicole, who got a call from her son's school one morning, asking her to come to the school because her son was disrupting class. She was furious, at both the school and teacher, for making her get off work. The fact that she herself was a teacher meant that she, of all people, should know better, but teacher does not trump being a human being and a mother, so off she went: good teacher to do battle with bad, incompetent, unfit to be a janitor teacher. She is escorted to the child's room and peers into the little classroom window before storming in to tell the incompetent off, when she spots her son. I Quote here. "He was standing on top of the desk, acting like a stone fool." Welcome to the wonderful world of the teacher. Nicole said that she became a good parent that day. Let the teachers do their jobs. DO NOT PROTECT YOUR CHILD FROM THE CONSEQUENCES OF THEIR OWN MISBEHAVIOR or else they will never learn anything. You will be backing down the teacher, then backing down the administrators, then backing down the police officer, then backing down the probation officer and then you are going to be trying to back down the state prosecutor, who apparently doesn't know what back down means. He is a dolt. And you have lost your child forever. This can all be avoided. Do not shield your child from deserved punishment.

The last thing you do as a good parent is to hand your parent role to other good adults that are in your child's life and let them do their best. Have faith. My son called me from school one time, explaining that he had after school detention. I said "Oh?" and picked him up after school. I asked him why I was being asked to spend my valuable time being chauffeur and his explanation went like this: "Dad, the teacher is such a jerk. Nobody likes him." I said, "What did the jerk ask you to do?" "He asked me to stop talking during class. But......." "Did you, in fact, stop talking in class?" My son is a very bright child, bright enough to be a lawyer. He could sense that his case was going south at light speed. "No. But everybody else was talking and nobody was paying attention to the man any and.............". At this time his voice was trailing off into nothingness. If you are a good teacher you don't need words to convey complex meaning. The proper stare with the proper attitude will suffice nicely. I am a particularly good teacher. Once he was silent I decided to speak. "Son, you know I love you. You are going to be a great chef when you get older, just as you say you are. I have one word of advice. If a teacher-even the most incompetent, lame, drooling, foolish, ignorant, boring and detestable joke of a teacher on the planet-one who in fact forged his teacher certificate- asks you to do anything, up to and including setting your hair on fire, you are going to do it. DO YOU UNDERSTAND ME? As I have said before, children are sensitive and have an uncanny ability to pick up the most subtle of messages. All I know is that I never got a call from the school again.

The thing about being overprotective is the silent message that you are sending to your child. It is that, in reality, you don't have faith that she can do anything on her own. If you keep hovering over her, you're probably right. Instead of being a launching pad to greatness, you will become a crutch, something to lean on while complaining about the day's failures. I still remember the day I got my first flat tire. I was in my teens and was out on a date. I was acting the big man until I heard the flopping of the tire and pulled over. My first instinct was to call Dad. I had gone from big man to medium sized boy in the blink of an eye. My father did me a huge favor that day. He told me where the jack was, then hung up. After a half an hour I was the big man again, to stay. False praise and overprotection does not instill a sense of man or womanhood. Concrete, actual successful accomplishments do. The more successful accomplishments that you can provide for your child as they are growing up, the more of a man or woman you will have later on in life.

So, now you have got the home thing and school thing going on. What can possibly derail your child from being a successful adult? He is bright, happy, intelligent, caring, self-motivated, so handsome that Denzel Washington or Richard Gere are jealous. What could possibly go wrong? The entire media empire set up to make money off of destroying your child is one thing. Another is their "friends" who have watched one video too many, drenched in sex, violence, disrespect, criminality and rampant materialism, until they think that this pirate fantasy world is real. And now they are your child's best friend. The parent's question is, who is going to influence whom?

This friend business is very important to study closely, because, after a certain age, the "friend" has a lot more influence on your child than you do. So, even though the child will scream with indignation that it is none of your business, press on with getting to know who these friends are, because it is in fact your most important business of the day. So, who does your child hang out with? You can tell a lot by checking out their aforementioned tattoos. Does the tattoo have meaning? Does it look like a doctor bending over a microscope doing cancer research, or does it lean more towards a dagger inserted through a skull? Is it a cute butterfly placed strategically on the lower back or is it a mural of snakes eating infants displayed across the chest and down both arms? These give a clue as to a person's outlook on life. Devils anywhere on the body, no matter how minute, are a bad sign. Hair styles are another clue, but murkier to read. Every generation goes through phases guaranteed to drive the previous generation crazy. I can live with the hair thing. I remember when my uncle came home with a Mohawk haircut once. My grandfather, who was a career military man, was not amused. Upon threats of death my uncle changed his hairstyle. He came back with a Cossack, which is a shrunk up version of the Mohawk, and looks even worse. A lot of the black kids at school used to cut their initials in their hair. I have a high tolerance for strange hair, as long as it doesn't show disrespect. If the letters in their head didn't spell a word that is banned off the public airwaves, I could live with it if their parents could. One time my son came with his mother, sporting a brand new haircut called the rat tail. How fitting.

Drug abuse is a whole different ball game. Watch how your child acts while waiting for their "friend" to arrive. If they are calmly doing their homework, that is one thing. If they are continuously rocking back and forth like the pitching coach Leo Mazzoni in the ninth inning, that is not good. If they are chewing on their hand and making growling sounds, you better hope their friend gets there quick.

Know who your child's friends are. And know where they are. Don't win the trifecta like a frantic parent who returned a call to me at the school. Her son had been skipping and I wanted to know what was up. She said that she hadn't seen her son in two weeks. He was living somewhere, and I am not making this up, "down the street with a kid that she couldn't remember the name of, except that his nickname was "Spider".

What happens when there is no real functioning family unit at the house? The child will create his own family unit, except without the word functioning anywhere to be seen. This family is called a gang. The desire to belong is almost as strong as the desire to eat, and a child will belong to something, somewhere. The children who are so alienated that they actually feel that they don't belong ANYWHERE are the ones who shoot the school up. I suggest that you do everything in your power to make that child feel like a productive member of a FAMILY. If they are a member of a family, then you have certain rights as a parent, like the right to ask "where are you going, who with, what are you planning on doing and when are you getting home?" The decibel level of their shrieking will inform you of how tight of a leash you need to keep on them so that they will survive long enough to become that successful adult that you keep harping about.

    I was reading an article about the movie star Al Pacino. It stated that he grew up in a tough neighborhood and was often angry at his mother because, in his mind, she was the worst mother on the planet. Instead of letting little Al go outside and play with his hoodlum friends she insisted on him staying inside and completing his schoolwork. This set Al up for years of ridicule. He was a sissy boy and his mother was a domineering, pig headed old witch. Al the movie star will tell you this: Many of those friends who kept yelling for him to come out and play are either dead or in jail. Al Pacino the movie star would not exist today if it wasn't for a mother who was stronger and more focused than most. Mr. Pacino knows this. He said that she saved his life. It is how you raise your child when they are very young, and the parent-child RELATIONSHIP and bond that you develop early that will allow both parent and child to survive the teenage years.

    There you have it. It's two o'clock. Time sure does fly when you're having fun. Before you go, I want to say a couple of things to you personally. You are all good kids. I can tell by the look in your eyes. Don't have children before you are ready. I'm not worried about the fate of the babies right now. I am worried about your fate. There is so much potential for greatness in this room. Some of you will end up saving lives in your various professions. Your greatness knows no boundaries. You can destroy all that in one single unguarded moment. If you have a child too early, YOUR LIFE AS YOU KNOW IT IS OVER. Altered forever. And you will spend the rest of it trying to dig yourself and your child out of a poverty hole. That is going to be a tough climb. Respect yourself. Have faith in yourself. You deserve better than that. The world deserves better than that. It needs your greatness today, more so than ever before. Be there to meet your destiny. Don't take yourself out of the picture. Be there when it is your time. And parent smartly so that your child will be there when it is their time. May God bless you and help you make good choices. Enjoy the rest of your weekend. It has been my pleasure to have been here today.

For information on speaking engagements contact
Bill Hoatson at:

P.O. Box 302, Greensboro, FL 32330
or
hoatson@worldnet.att.net